IRAN II
PERSIEN II
PERSIA II

MEXICO	Jacques Soustelle
PERSIA I (From the origins to the Achaemenids)	Jean-Louis Huot, Agrégé of the University; Member of the French Institute of Archaeology of Beirut
PERU	Rafael Larco Hoyle†, Director of the Rafael Larco Herrera Museum, Lima
PREHISTORY	Denise de Sonneville-Bordes, Ph. D.
ROME	Gilbert Picard, Professor at the Sorbonne, Paris
SOUTH CAUCASUS	Boris B. Piotrovsky, Director of the Hermitage Museum, Leningrad
SOUTH SIBERIA	Mikhail Gryaznov, Professor at the Archaeological Institute of Leningrad
SYRIA-PALESTINE I (Ancient Orient)	Jean Perrot, Head of the French Archaeological Mission in Israel
SYRIA-PALESTINE II (Classical Orient)	Michael Avi Yonah, Professor at the Hebrew University of Jerusalem
THE TEUTONS	R. Hachmann, Professor at the University of Saarbrücken
URARTU	Boris B. Piotrovsky, Director of the Hermitage Museum, Leningrad

ARCHAEOLOGIA
MVNDI

Series prepared under the direction of Jean
Marcadé, Professor of Archaeology at the
University of Bordeaux

VLADIMIR G. LUKONIN

PERSIA II

Translated from the Russian by JAMES HOGARTH

76 illustrations in colour; 141 illustrations in black and white

THE WORLD PUBLISHING COMPANY CLEVELAND
AND NEW YORK

CONTENTS

PREFACE

Among historians of ancient Iran the Hellenistic period and early Middle Age have a well-earned reputation for obscurity and confusion. In order to bring some order out of the confusion there is a strong temptation to simplify the pattern by reducing it to its broadest lines, and this has led to a proliferation of theories and hypotheses. But there is perhaps a more scientific approach to these problems, and one which may, if we are fortunate, enable us to solve them. This is to appeal to archaeology for the exact information which is lacking in the written sources, building up our picture by a careful sifting of the new evidence—incomplete, perhaps, but unimpeachable—which is provided by excavation.

Archaeology is thought of as an auxiliary science to history; but in this role it is not concerned merely to accumulate a mass of interesting or valuable objects. Its task is to understand and interpret this material. After classifying its finds according to their relationships and associations, and if possible dating them by independent evidence, with the aid of its own specialised techniques, it must then seek to analyse the essential content of the various objects and other remains, to understand their purpose and significance, and to establish their value as evidence of a particular civilisation, as well as to appreciate their artistic merits. It must be the aim of archaeology to assess the full implications of these things against the background of the political and social system, the economic and commercial organisation, and the forms of worship and religious conceptions of the period and the society which produced them.

The absorbing interest of Vladimir Lukonin's work lies in its demonstration, on the basis of some typical examples, of how the archaeologist becomes a historian without leaving his own speciality, using only the material which it is his special province to study—whether tiny objects like the coins and seals or huge monuments like the rock carvings. The conclusions to which he leads us are of great interest; and we are grateful also for the opportunity he gives us to admire so many splendid works from the Hermitage Museum.

J.M

We should like to express our gratitude to Professor B.B. Piotrovsky, Director of the Hermitage Museum, Leningrad, without whose ready cooperation the production of this book would not have been possible. We are grateful also to the Director General of Antiquities in the Ministry of Culture, Baghdad, and to Mr A. Pourmand, Director General of the Archaeological Service of Iran, who have been of great assistance to us in the selection of illustrations.

Our thanks are also due to Messrs Niklaus Dürr, Principal Keeper in the Museum of Art and History, Geneva, Georges Le Rider, Keeper in the Cabinet des Médailles, Paris, and Professor Georges Redard, of the University of Berne, who have given us much valuable help and advice.

Finally we should like to express our sincere appreciation to Their Excellencies General Hassan Pakravan, Iranian Ambassador to Pakistan, Dr Ghassem Rezai, Director of the Iranian National Tourist Organisation, and Professor and Mrs Mohsen Moghadam of Teheran, who are always generous with their help in any of our publications concerned with Iran.

INTRODUCTION

It is the object of this book to introduce the reader to the problems, methods and results of the archaeology of Iran over a period of something like a thousand years. The story is necessarily a complicated one, for we are concerned not with a single period but with a succession of periods which externally appear very different but internally are closely linked with one another. These are periods exposed to the full light of history, for which we have a considerable volume of contemporary evidence and many remains of culture and art; periods, therefore, about which we apparently know a good deal. Through the narrative of the Roman soldier and writer Ammianus Marcellinus, for example, we can follow day by day the desperate and gruelling war between Persia and Rome in the months of April to June in the year 363 A.D., and obtain a clear picture not only of the tortuous manœuvres of the Emperor Julian the Apostate and the King of Kings Shapur II but of the tactics and equipment employed, the court intrigues, and the characters of the commanders. Reading Plutarch, we can visualise the scene in the theatre of the Armenian city of Artaxata (Artashat) when the actors, speaking the well-known lines from the *Bacchae* of Euripides—"Thus we bring from distant mountains, soaked in gore, our glorious prey"—produced before the ruler of Persia, Orodes, the bloody head of Caesar's ally, the triumvir Marcus Crassus, an ambitious man but an incompetent general.

It may seem, therefore, that the whole course of this civilisation is clear and comprehensible; that we have only to bring together all the written sources and the period will come alive before our eyes in its natural colours; that the material remains of its culture which now adorn our museums are simply illustrations to the story recorded by contemporary writers; and that the function of archaeology is merely to provide a commentary on the written sources. This may be our first impression; but in fact the matter is very much more complicated than this. The written sources left by the Persians themselves are extremely fragmentary. For the period of almost five hundred years during which the Parthian empire existed (from 250 B.C. to the third decade of the 3rd century A.D.) we have only a few administrative documents on parchment, some two thousand ostraca (inscribed sherds) with records of the delivery of wine to one of the properties of the King of Kings, and a handful of official inscriptions. We are rather better supplied with documentary evidence in the following period, that of the Sassanid dynasty (from the third decade of the 3rd century to 651 A.D.); our material for this period includes not only business documents and official inscriptions but also religious texts (or at any rate fragments of such texts) and literary works.

Yet few in number as the documents are, they require much concentrated work by philologists, linguists, palaeographers and historians: the reading of almost every one of them involves a laborious process of decipherment.

The language of administration in the Achaemenian chancelleries was not the Old Persian cuneiform, but the Aramaic language which was the *lingua franca* of the Empire. All documents, therefore, were written in this language; and the practice of the Achaemenian chancelleries was followed in later periods. The rulers of the Seleucid dynasty maintained the old Achaemenian system and proclaimed Aramaic, along with Greek, the official language of their empire, thereby artificially inhibiting the creation of alphabets for the Iranian languages.

In those areas where no similar edict was issued the local languages were not long in creating their own alphabet, and the Aramaic language was fairly rapidly eliminated. Thus, for example, an Indian inscription by Asoka (Maurya dynasty) which was discovered at Pul-i Darunta in Afghanistan is, formally, in Aramaic, but the Prakrit words which it contains are not merely accepted local terms but represent an attempt to write the local language in the Aramaic alphabet. Soon there appeared in north-western India the Kharosthi script, based on Aramaic but adapted to meet the requirements of the local tongue. By about 200 B.C. the Aramaic language had disappeared from the whole of the Middle East and been superseded by Kharosthi.

The situation was very different in Iran. We may take as an example a group of documents from a wine store at Mihrdatkart, written in the 1st century B.C. These are the so-called Nisa ostraca, about which we shall have more to say later.

The following, transliterated into the Latin alphabet, is the text of one of these documents:
BHWTH ZNH MN pryptykn MN KRM' 'wzbry ZYLYD PHT 'Hm XXII HYTY srwšyk W mytry mdwbr ZY MN 'rg... HN'Lt ŠNT II C X III III

This may be translated as follows:
"In this vessel from Phriapatikan, from the tribute-paying vineyard which is at the disposal of the satrap, of wine 22 *mari* (a measure of capacity). (It) was brought by Sroshak and Mihr, wine stewards from the region of 'rg... (the name of the region or place is partly obliterated). Brought for the year 216 (according to the Arsacid era, i.e., 32 B.C.)."

In what language is this document written? All the words shown in capitals in the transliteration are Aramaic, and only the place names, personal names and titles ("wine stewards") are written in Persian, in Aramaic letters. Nevertheless the document is a Persian one: this is shown not only by the names but also by the fact that the Aramaic verb (HN'L) has the so-called Persian "phonetic complement" indicating its person and number.

This confused system of writing—almost as if the message were in code—developed because the Persian scribes of the period, following the traditions of the Achaemenian chancelleries, frequently used Aramaic words and even whole phrases, which for them had become standard formulae. Texts of this kind are called heterographic, and in reading them we are always faced with the problem of deciding how to read a particular group of letters—as a hete-rogram (an Aramaic word) or as an "open spelling" (a Persian word)—and whether to read a particular document in Aramaic or in Persian. It is clear that the meaning of the text will vary according to our choice. Consider, for example, the following two different readings of a document from Nisa.

The first reading is the work of the German scholar Franz Altheim, who decided that the text was written in Aramaic and interpreted it as: "Eutychius. From the master we shall bring to thee, and he shall receive 206." The second reading, by the Soviet scholars I. M. Dyakonov and V. A. Livshits, to whom belongs the credit of deciphering the whole of the Nisa records, is: "In this vessel from the tribute-paying vineyard named Hindukan, of wine 16 *mari*."

Difficulties of this kind, added to the scantiness of our stock of authentic documents and inscriptions, compel us to depend very largely on the ancient authors, the fragmentary references in the works of Armenian, Syrian and Byzantine historians, and the much later works written or compiled during the Arab dominance in Iran but preserving ancient, though badly distorted, traditions. Accordingly the history of Iran in the period with which we are concerned is like a mosaic which has been put together from a great many small pieces, but which still contains many blank spaces.

In the formation of this mosaic a very important part is played by the archaeogical monuments and the material remains of Iranian culture.

THE HISTORICAL BACKGROUND

Alexander of Macedon died in Babylon in 323 B.C., too soon to see the fruits of his policy. In spite of the hundreds of cities similar to the cities of the Greeks which had been founded throughout his vast empire, in spite of the numerous marriages between his closest associates and his soldiers and women of the ancient local dynasties and nobility, despite all his efforts to establish a uniform system of law, Alexander had not succeeded in achieving the cultural and economic unity of his domains.

Political Developments

After the death of its founder the great empire collapsed, and there followed a long period of wars between the Diadochi, the Successors. The satrapies of the empire were shared out between Alexander's generals, changing hands time and time again, until at last two of his commanders, Seleucus and Ptolemy, established their dominance over the others. Ptolemy gained possession of Egypt and founded a dynasty which was to rule over the country for more than three hundred years. Seleucus, having conquered almost all Alexander's possessions in Asia, and gained control for a time of all the territory from the coast of Asia Minor to India, established a kingdom no less extensive than the Achaemenid Empire. In the reigns of Seleucus's immediate successors, however, a number of provinces and satrapies fell away, and the only areas which his descendants were able to hold on to for any length of time were a few districts in Mesopotamia and western Iran.

One of the satrapies which declared its independence only seventy years after Alexander's death was Parthia or Parthyene. About the year 250 the nomadic Parni, pushing into the regions along the south-eastern shores of the Caspian (the valley of the river Atrek), proclaimed one of their leaders, Arshak (Arsaces), as king. Soon not only Parthia itself but also Hyrcania and other areas in the north-east of Iran were under Arshak's control. The prospect of losing the eastern satrapies gradually developed into the prospect that the whole of Iran might be lost to the Greeks. By 200 B.C. the Parthian rulers had firmly established themselves in north-western Iran, and fifty years later the Parthian King Mithridates I captured the Seleucid capital, Seleuceia on Tigris, and was proclaimed ruler of Babylonia (141 B.C.).

The power of the Greeks was now declining. In spite of the fact that the Parthians had to face constant pressure from the nomadic tribes in the East, in spite of the heroic efforts of one of the last Seleucid rulers, Antiochus VII Sidetes, to save his kingdom by a decisive battle in Media, the fall of the Seleucids was inevitable. After the defeat of Antiochus Parthia became a world power. Its territory extended from Mesopotamia to the Amu-Darya, and the Parthian ruler Mithridates II (123–87 B.C.), the first of the "Arsacid" dynasty, who took the title of King of Kings, put his protégé Tigranes II on the throne of Armenia and thus gained the opportunity of intervening in the play of political forces as far afield as Asia Minor. The Seleucid Empire, now confined to an area in northern Syria, lost all further influence on the course of history, and Parthia for the first time came into conflict with the interests of Rome. The two great world powers, having advanced their armies to the Euphrates, now prepared themselves for the decisive struggle for control of the whole of the Near East.

And then, on 6th May in the year 53 B.C., there took place near Carrhae in northern Mesopotamia the famous battle between the Parthians and the Romans which is so vividly described by Plutarch. At the head of the Roman legions was Marcus Crassus, a rich and ambitious man but a poor general. He dreamed of repeating the exploits of Alexander and advancing with his army to India, and he dreamed also of the fantastic riches of the East. His troops, exhausted by a senseless and gruelling march across the steppes of Mesopotamia, were attacked by the armour-clad Parthian cavalry. The defeat of the Romans was crushing: some twenty thousand Roman soldiers fell in the battle and some ten thousand were taken prisoner. Their leader, Marcus Crassus, committed suicide.

The battle of Carrhae finally put an end to Rome's hopes of becoming sole mistress of the Near East. Henceforth the frequent skirmishes in frontier areas no longer had much effect on the political map.

In 20 B.C. Augustus concluded peace with the Parthian King Phraates IV and stabilised the position. From this time onwards, in spite of internal disturbances and continual court intrigues in Parthia, and repeated attempts by Rome to capture territory in Mesopotamia—during the 2nd century A.D. there were ten or twelve military campaigns—both states broadly preserved their existing boundaries.

Internal processes which were taking place in Parthia, however—the dissolution of the commune as the basis of society, the crisis of the slave-owning system, the disturbance to international transit trade as a result of the never-ending wars in Mesopotamia (the economic heart of the empire) and on the eastern frontiers, and the sharp decline in the economy—brought the Parthian empire to the point of catastrophe. The final decline of this world power, further weakened as it was by continual dynastic quarrels, was one symptom of the general crisis which affected all the countries of the Mediterranean basin at the beginning of the 3rd century.

The Parthian empire now lingered on, broken up into a patchwork of semi-independent states. Rome's enemy lay impotent before her: it seemed that only one more blow was needed and the fate of the Near East would be decided for many years to come. This was no doubt the opinion of Alexander Severus, the general in command of the Roman army in Mesopotamia, who had led his troops to the Euphrates. But there the legionaries met the Persian cavalry and, to their surprise, saw in front of them not a few disorganised units led by commanders who spent their time intriguing against one another, but a formidable army. In the year 235 the Romans suffered their first defeat at the hands of a Persian army led by a King of Kings belonging to a new dynasty, Ardashir, a descendant of Sassan; and twenty-five years later, at a battle near Carrhae, where Marcus Crassus had fallen, the Persians captured the Roman Emperor Valerian. Iran was once again united into a powerful empire, the lost territory in Mesopotamia was recovered, and the enfeebled power of Rome was now confronted by the vigorous young empire of the Sassanids.

In the year 227 Ardashir, king of Fars (southern Iran), having gathered his strength and defeated the last king of the Parthian dynasty, Artabanus V, at Hormizdagan, had proclaimed himself King of Kings of Iran. This was more than a mere dynastic change. At a time of acute social crisis in the Mediterranean and Asia Minor, when the elements of a feudal society were developing in the Parthian empire, the coming to power of a new national dynasty, which proclaimed as one of its aims the "restoration" of the ancient national and religious traditions and was supported by the nobility and priesthood, meant the beginning of a new stage in the history of Iran, the period known as the "early Middle Age" *(Plates 108-112)*.

The four hundred and fifty years of the Sassanid dynasty are usually represented in Persian historiography and literature as a brilliant period in which culture and art flourished, the period of the "national revival of Iran", an age of powerful rulers, learned scholars and poets. And indeed there is much truth in this picture. At war with Rome, and later with Byzantium, in the west, and under constant pressure from the nomads in the east, the Sassanid rulers nevertheless created a vast empire which at one time (in the 6th century A.D.) extended as far as Egypt. But acute social conflicts, in particular the rising of the urban poor and the peasantry under the leadership of Mazdak in the 6th century—the largest rising of its kind in the Near East—shattered the economic foundations of the state, and the Sassanian empire fell to the attacks of the Arab cavalry between the thirties and the fifties of the 7th century.

The Social and Economic Context

Before concluding this account of the main events in the history of Iran during a period of a thousand years I should like to summarise, in the most general terms, the internal development of the country, basing myself on the written sources, mainly on the Eastern sources written in Aramaic (one of the official languages of the Seleucid and Parthian empires), Pahlavi (the Persian language of the Parthian period) and "Middle Persian" (the language of the Sassanian period). The following few pages have a double aim—not only to discuss the internal development of Iran, but also to give some idea of the nature of the local (Persian) written records.

The Towns

The Seleucid and Parthian empires were a medley of different peoples, customs, beliefs and languages. The economic life of the country was based on a number of different patterns: in the economic heart of the country, Mesopotamia, there was an advanced slave-owning system, but in the central areas and in the East more primitive forms of economy prevailed. In these circumstances the towns were of predominant importance.

The story of the rise of the towns is perhaps the most striking, the most troubled and the most significant page in the economic history of the East. In the Seleucid period, after the conquests of Alexander, there arose in the East a number of self-governing cities, the *poleis*. But self-government of this kind had been known even before the time of Alexander. Babylon, Nippur, Ur, Eridu and other cities of the Assyrian Empire, for example, were urban communities centred on the local temples, the inhabitants of which enjoyed certain privileges. The whole earlier development of Iran had prepared it for the adoption of the *polis* system. In the Hellenistic period, however—a period marked by the economic isolation of the various regions and the increasing centralisation of state authority—the *polis* was the form of organisation which allowed greatest scope for slave ownership, by hindering the intervention of the king or the priesthood in the affairs of the slave-owning estates. On the other hand the *poleis* were a source of strength to the central government, bringing the extensive territories attached to the cities under the authority of the Hellenistic kings, and punctually paying into the royal treasury the appropriate share of the revenue produced by these territories.

The existence of the *poleis* ensured the political unity of the country, and many new cities were therefore founded in the Seleucid period—Antiochia in Persis, Nihavend, a number of Seleuceias, etc. Sometimes the privileges of a *polis* were granted to a *katoikia*—a military colony in which the settlers received grants of land and were obliged in return to give military service. In some cases cities were founded in order to establish new organisms closely associated with the ruling dynasty in opposition to the ancient communities centred on the temples: the town of Dura-Europos on the Euphrates, for example, was a foundation of this kind. Sometimes a number of communities combined to form a town, which was then granted the privileges of a Hellenistic *polis*: an example of this was the town of Susa, which became a *polis* in the reign of Seleucus II. A typical instance of the foundation of a *polis* of this kind is the town of Karka de bet Selokh, or Kirkuk. The chronicles of this city record that "Seleucus... divided (the town) into seventy-two streets and brought five well-known families from Istakhr, settling them there along with other people whom he brought from various places. To these five families he gave land and vineyards, and Karka was relieved of the obligation to pay taxes. Twelve streets were named after twelve well-known families, and the others were named after different crafts."

All these cities controlled a given territory. They were governed by assemblies of citizens, who elected the city council and the city magistrates. These elected officers controlled all the internal affairs of the city, but there also resided in the cities royal officials, the *epistatai*, who represented the authority of the king. The king conveyed his directions to the cities by means of special messages. In the course of time the royal officials steadily increased their influence over these towns, and the king's letters to the towns became steadily firmer and more pressing. A frequently quoted example of such a message is a letter written by the Parthian king Artabanus III to the city of

Susa (22 A.D.), in which he insistently urges the city council to elect the same person for the second time to the office of treasurer, although the city's constitution required that there should be an interval of not less than three years before an official was re-elected. The candidate for re-election, one Hestiaeus, belonged to the "imperial party"—that is, the section of the local nobility who supported the king.

What was the fate of these cities in the early Middle Age? Their economic basis, slave ownership, was destroyed, and the extent of the king's intervention in their affairs continually increased. The external forms of organisation, of course, persisted for some considerable time: we know, for example, that Susa lost its right of self-government only in the 4th century. The development of new social relationships, however, led to the supersession of these cities by towns of an entirely different type, which served as bases or strong points in the territories belonging to the imperial domain of the King of Kings.

The Sassanid monarchs, as they advanced into Mesopotamia—with the object not only of conquering territory but of maintaining the newly conquered areas within their empire—incorporated their conquests in their personal domain. The main bulwarks of the imperial power of the King of Kings became the cities bearing his name and governed by his officials. In Antioch, Tarsus, Caesarea and other cities conquered in the reign of Shapur I the temples of the city's gods—the worship of whom bound the citizens together—were thrown down and Zoroastrianism, the faith of the King of Kings, was implanted by force.

On the evidence of the written sources, the Sassanid Shahanshahs founded large numbers of cities. Thus Shapur I, the conqueror of the Roman Emperors Gordian, Philip the Arab and Valerian, won over large areas in Mesopotamia and established some dozen or more cities—Weh Antiok Shapur ("the better Antioch of Shapur"), Peroz Shapur ("the victory of Shapur"),

Tahm Shapur, etc. At the court of Shapur I there were fifteen "shahrabs" or stewards of the imperial cities. One of these was Rashn, shahrab of the city of Dura-Europos, which was now transformed into an imperial city and perhaps re-named. Part of the land attached to the city was granted to Persian settlers. The documents from the governor's chancellery, executive directions addressed to a variety of different people, give us some idea of the administrative organisation of cities of this type. The whole economic and administrative authority in the city was vested in the shahrab, and his authority extended also to a large area surrounding the city, the revenue from which was paid into the royal treasury. Attached to the shahrab's chancellery were a steward of the area, with a large staff of clerks headed by a chief clerk, the commander of the armed forces stationed in the town, and a judge.

The Imperial Domain and Conditional Ownership of Land
The "imperial domain" was the second economic bulwark of the Hellenistic monarchies. The king's possessions (which may have been known as *ostâns* in the Parthian period) were extensive, particularly in Mesopotamia. Within these great territories, both in the Seleucid period and later, the kings designated particular areas on which they established cities (the Hellenistic *poleis*), thus converting part of the "imperial domain" into the property of the cities.

Our information about the management of the imperial domain comes from the records of the *madustân*, the wine stores of the imperial property of Mihrdatkart, the remains of which were found by the Southern Turkmenian Archaeological Expedition at the village of Bagir, near Ashkhabad. In this fortress were found the family burial-place of the Parthian kings, a number of temples, and various storehouses, including the *madustân*. The archaeologists who excavated it found over 2000 ostraca—pottery sherds, dating from the 1st century B.C., on which were inscribed in black ink records of the receipt of wine from various estates. On the evidence of these records the wine was delivered in considerable quantities from vineyards in the area belonging to the King of Kings and often bearing his name. The estates were his personal property, and the revenue from them went into the imperial treasury.

Sometimes parts of the imperial domain were granted to high dignitaries in a form of "conditional ownership". One such dignitary, Mnesimachus, who lived in the 3rd century B.C., was granted an estate which included an area of land in the village of Tobalmury, the peasants and slaves attached to the land, and two orchards. To these were added a number of fields for sowing and another orchard a short distance away, together with the slaves living on them.

We know about the property bestowed on Mnesimachus from an Aramaic parchment found at Dura-Europos. This shows that the king made the grant in recognition of Mnesimachus's management of an extensive imperial estate. We also know the conditions on which the land was granted to him: if the imperial domain to which it belonged was neglected, or if the revenue was not regularly remitted to the imperial treasury, Mnesimachus was to forfeit his property; and he was also forbidden to mortgage it.

The development of new social relationships in the Sassanian period necessarily changed the character of the imperial domain. Some of the newly conquered territories, particularly in western Iran, were now incorporated in the domain. Thus under the Sassanids the imperial domain was not reduced in size—as it was to some extent in the Seleucid and Parthian periods, when parts of the domain were assigned to the new cities—but rather increased: by abolishing the self-government of the existing towns, the king made these towns into bridgeheads of his authority throughout his domain, at the same time as he built new cities and renewed old ones.

Private Property; the Commune; Slave-Owning
During the Seleucid and Parthian periods there were large slave-owning estates in Mesopotamia. One of these estates, not far from Dura-Europos,

belonged to a certain Phraates, an important government official. In Dura-Europos the archaeologists found a promissory note ("Parchment No. X", dated 122 A.D.) recording that Phraates had advanced to a peasant named Barlaas, a member of a commune in the village of Paliga, on the security of his plot of land and all his other property, the sum of 400 silver drachmae. The document states that Barlaas, having received the loan, undertakes "until he shall have returned the sum advanced, to perform the service of a slave to him (Phraates),... doing all that shall be required of him,... being absent... neither by day nor by night." If Barlaas should be ill for longer than a week, and thus unable to work, he is to pay a penalty at the rate of a drachma for every day lost; and if he should seek refuge in the temple he is to be forcibly expelled. It is clear that when Barlaas or his fellow peasants were reduced to conditions like these they were in fact no better than slaves.

In 1909, in a cave near the small village of Avroman (Persian Kurdistan), some shepherds found a sealed pottery jar containing three parchments, two written in Greek and one in Aramaic; and within a very short period these documents, which were found to be contracts for the sale of a vineyard, were widely known and discussed.

All three documents bore dates: the first "in the month of Apellaeus in the year 225", the second "in the year 291", and the third "in the month of Arvatat in the year 300". All three were dated according to the Seleucid era: the date of the first was thus equivalent to 88 B.C., of the second to 22 or 21 B.C., and of the third—written in Aramaic—to 11 A.D.

The most interesting point was that all three contracts were concerned with the same plot of land, a vineyard, which over a period of just under a hundred years from the signing of the first contract changed hands at least three times. The first document records that two brothers, Baraces and Sobenes, are selling for 30 silver drachmae half a vineyard, the "personal allotment" assigned to them by the "owners of the adjacent land"—that is, the com-

2, 3→

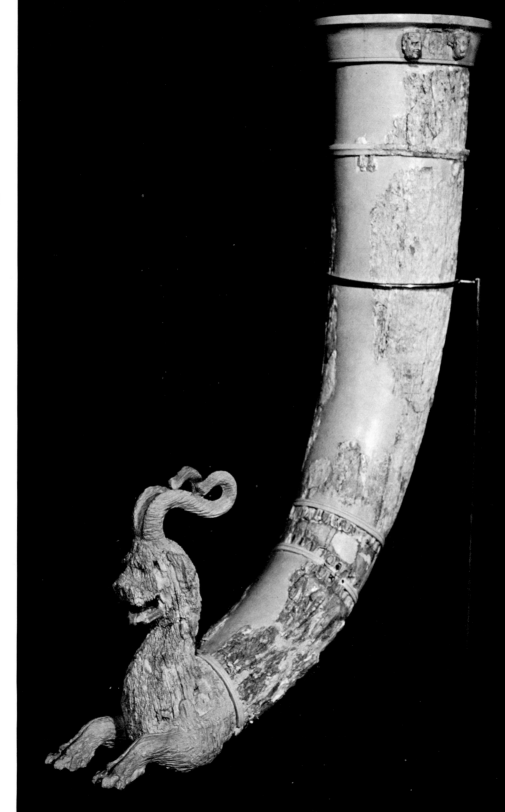

10

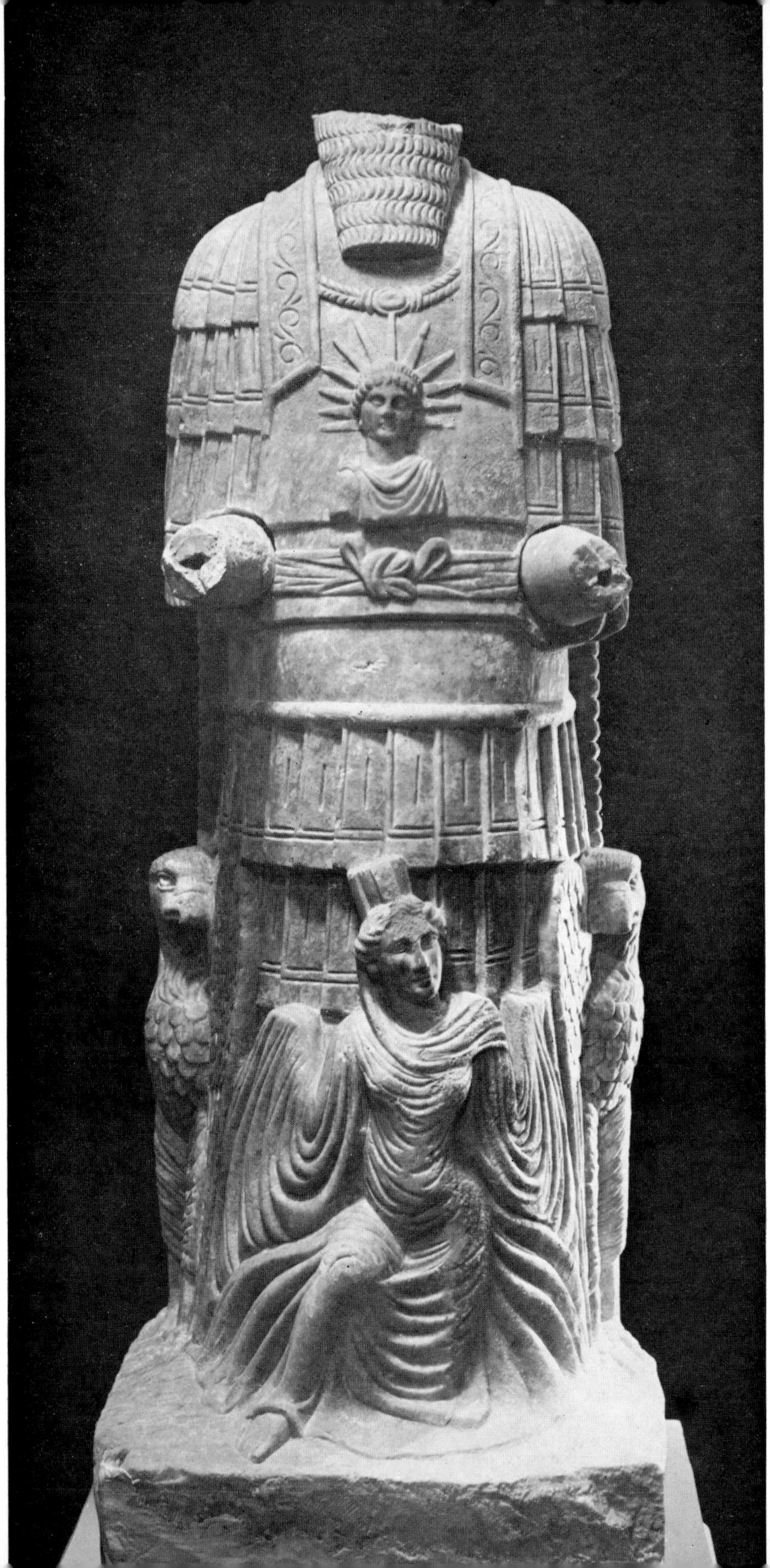

11

12

13

mune. We find almost exactly the same story in the other two documents, except that the owners are different and the price of the land has risen: by the year 11 A.D. the 30 drachmae have become 55.

It is interesting to note the conditions on which the land was sold. In the first document the purchaser, Gathaces, binds himself, along with Baraces and Sobenes, to pay the land tax due on the whole plot, and the owners of the plot are required to look after the land, to cultivate it properly, and to pay the tax regularly. If the conditions are not observed this is to be regarded as a breach of the contract and the offender is required, without further legal process, to suffer a penalty of 200 drachmae, and to pay a similar sum into the royal treasury. The penalty was thus more than seven times the value of the land.

The peasants belonging to the commune had their personal allotments of land and were permitted to sell them. They were required to pay an annual land tax in respect of their holdings, and this makes it necessary to suppose that both the areas of the plots and the amounts of tax due were recorded in registers of some kind. It appears from the documents, too, that the peasant belonging to a commune was attached to the land and was under obligation both to the commune and to the government to cultivate his plot and pay his land tax regularly. The documents found at Avroman had been carefully preserved by the peasants, for they established their ownership of the small vineyard which constituted their whole wealth. Misfortune or a poor harvest could involve them in the payment of a monetary penalty quite incommensurate with the value of their property: it may well be, indeed, that Barlaas borrowed the 400 silver drachmae from Phraates in order to save his land—which a peasant valued more highly than his own freedom—and to meet his obligations to the commune and the government.

When peasants belonging to a commune, like Barlaas, were ruined in this way they would work alongside the slaves on the estates of the nobility. We know something of the life of the slaves who worked on the imperial domain, on the estate of a landowner like Mnesimachus or on the property of a man like Phraates from various sources, and in particular from a Sassanian legal textbook—reflecting conditions dating back to the Parthian and early Sassanian periods—known as the "Collection of a Thousand Decisions". When a property was sold or otherwise transferred to a new owner the slaves were regarded as necessary equipment and passed with the land. This is recorded, for example, in one of the parchments found at Dura-Europos.

During the crisis of the 2nd and 3rd centuries there developed in slave-owning Mesopotamia the practice of partially liberating slaves attached to the land. According to legal documents of this period the slaves on many privately owned estates, while continuing to cultivate their masters' land, might be allowed a share of what they produced (in the form of part of the harvest or of their earnings) to the extent of between a quarter and a tenth of their output. This was clearly an attempt by some slave-owning landlords to find a solution to the crisis; and the process was considerably intensified under the early Sassanids.

The meagreness of our sources does not permit a detailed reconstruction of the economic life of Iran. We know, for example, that large landed properties were owned by the great noble families of Iran—the Surens (who possessed certain areas in Seistan), the Karens (whose estates were near Nihavend), the Spahpats (who owned Dihistan and Gurgan), and others. The representatives of these families of the high nobility—the ancient aristocracy of Iran—also occupied dominating positions in the government of the country. The economic relationships which prevailed on their estates can, however, be deduced only from the analogy of other regions in Iran. We also know very little about the property which belonged to the various temples. On the analogy of an earlier period we may suppose that the temples owned extensive properties in land and played an important part in the economy of the country. But on all these matters the available sources throw little light.

THE CONTRIBUTION
OF ARCHAEOLOGY

II

The archaeology of Iran in the Seleucid, Parthian and Sassanian periods is a discipline of very recent growth. The monuments of these periods have long been known in Europe: thus one of Sir John Chardin's companions, Grelot, left a very accurate sketch of the rock carvings by the Parthian King Mithridates II at Behistun, which he had visited in the year 1673. His drawing is a document of outstanding importance, for the carvings were soon afterwards almost completely destroyed. Karsten Niebuhr, who visited Iran in the early sixties of the 18th century, also brought back drawings of rock carvings of the Sassanian period and copies of inscriptions. His sketches, in fact, provided the basis for the decipherment of the Middle Persian inscriptions by Silvestre de Sacy, so that scholars were able to interpret the inscriptions of the Parthian and Sassanian periods before they could read the Old Persian cuneiform. The British architect Sir Robert Ker Porter, who was an excellent draughtsman, visited Iran in the early years of the 19th century and produced a large volume illustrated by his sketches of many archaeological monuments of the Parthian and Sassanian periods *(Plates 126, 130, 131)*.

Archaeologists and Excavators

In the 19th century, however—the golden age of Near Eastern archaeology—the archaeologists excavating ancient cities and settlements paid little or no attention to the Seleucid, Parthian and Sassanian levels, being concerned to reach as soon as possible the levels containing works of art of the Babylonian, Assyrian and Achaemenian periods. From the point of view of the archaeology of Iran in the Hellenistic period and the early Middle Age the excavations of the French archaeological expedition to Susa (end of 19th century) were particularly disastrous, almost completely destroying the important Seleucid and Parthian levels. Until comparatively recent times archaeologists were firmly convinced that the monuments of the material culture of Iran in the Parthian period were alien elements, outside the mainstream of development of Iranian art, and therefore unworthy of attention; and many masterpieces of Iranian artistic craftsmanship belonging to these periods were attributed to the civilisation of the Mediterranean and regarded as examples of the "Roman provincial style".

It was not until the early twenties of this century that the problems connected with the culture of Iran in the Parthian and Sassanian periods began to attract serious attention from scholars. Henceforth new features were continually appearing on the archaeological map; in the great museums of the world whole sections were devoted to the monuments of these periods; and works on the archaeology of Iran were no longer complete without chapters on these "dark ages".

Some Great Names

In the archaeology of Iran in this period particular credit is due to Sir Aurel Stein, among whose most striking discoveries were the Parthian temple at Shami (Khuzistan), with its famous bronze statues, and the remains of the great city of Kuh-i Khwaja, situated on an island in Lake Hamun in Seistan. Stein's work was continued by Ernst Herzfeld, a scholar who opened up a whole new period of archaeology. His *Archäologische Mitteilungen aus Iran*— a dozen or so volumes concerned with the most varied aspects of the archaeology of Iran—seem to me the most characteristic of his many works. Herzfeld—a linguist and palaeographer, equally at home in ancient and modern tongues, an excellent architect and draughtsman, a historian of the widest interests and a skilled archaeologist—poured out in his works a great flood of new ideas: sometimes over-daring, sometimes too hastily arrived at, but always stimulating in their novelty and unexpectedness. All subsequent study of the culture of Iran in the Hellenistic period and the early Middle Age has been inspired by these ideas. Herzfeld carried out the excavation of the Neolithic settlement on the terrace of Persepolis, excavated the Achaemenian capital of Persepolis and Pasargadae, continued Sir Aurel Stein's work at Kuh-i Khwaja, carried out a meticulous study of the art of Iran from the earliest times to the Middle Age, conducted brilliant excavations at Samarra, and studied the architectural monuments of the early Islamic period. It is probably true to say that he never visited any remains of the past of Iran without writing at least a few pages to record his impressions and conclusions. He also produced the first serious general study of the archaeology of Iran, the course of lectures published in 1935 under the title of the *Archaeological History of Iran (Plates 13, 21, 28)*.

Another outstanding student of this period was Professor M. I. Rostovtzeff—an archaeologist who carried out the systematic excavation of the city of Dura-Europos on the Euphrates, an art historian and a student of the economic and social conditions of the Hellenistic period. Rostovtzeff was the first to pose, and to a large extent to solve, the problem of the art of Parthia—in his classic essay, *Dura and the Problem of Parthian Art*, one of the foundations of the study of the Hellenistic period in the East.

The Main Hellenistic Sites

By the early thirties of this century scholars had available to them a number of outstanding monuments of the Hellenistic period. The most interesting of these was the city of Dura-Europos on the Euphrates, first discovered in 1920 when, in the course of military operations against rebellious Arabs, a detachment under the command of Captain Murphy occupied a group of nondescript ruins on the banks of the Euphrates. While digging trenches in the ruins the troops suddenly came upon fragments of wall paintings in an excellent state of preservation. It was later established that their trenches had cut through a temple dedicated to the "divine triad" of Palmyra, the gods Malakhbel, Aglibol and Jahribol. Captain Murphy reported his discovery to the Department of Antiquities of Iraq, and the site was examined by the well-known American Egyptologist Professor James Breasted, who submitted a report on the wall paintings to the French Académie des Inscriptions et Belles-Lettres.

To Franz Cumont, who came to Dura-Europos with an archaeological expedition in 1923, it was clear from the outset that in these wall paintings the learned world was confronted with an entirely new and unexpected line of development in the art of the East. The figures in their stiff hieratic poses, the enormous eyes staring into the distance on which the whole attention of the artist seemed to have been concentrated, the whole pattern of life represented in the paintings, the strange costume worn by the people, the various attributes which accompanied them: all this pointed, on the one hand, to the relative antiquity of the frescoes, and on the other was strangely reminiscent of Christian art. It was significant that the first archaeologist to see the paintings, Breasted, entitled his study of them *Oriental Forerunners of Byzantine Painting.*

Cumont's expedition worked for only three seasons. It was an unsettled period, and the excavations had to be carried on under the protection of soldiers. But even the modest results achieved aroused so much interest that excavations were resumed in 1928, this time with financial support from the University of Yale, under the leadership of Professor Rostovtzeff of that University, who remained in charge until his death.

Dura-Europos and Mesopotamia

The history of the town is still known only in its broad lines. It was founded about the year 300 B.C. as a Seleucid city, a manifestation of the policy of "urbanisation" pursued by the Seleucid monarchs. Dura-Europos was not only a caravan city on the route linking Syria and Persia but also a military outpost of the Greeks, and later the Romans, on the Euphrates. Its population included not only Greeks but also Palmyrenes, Syrians and Arabs. In the 2nd century barracks for the Roman garrison were built in the city. Finally, after an existence of five hundred years, Dura-Europos was taken by storm in 256 A.D. by the armies of the Sassanid King of Kings Shapur I and was destroyed.

The results of the excavations at Dura-Europos led to a striking increase in our knowledge of practically every branch of archaeology. They revealed the principles of the local style of architecture and the plans of houses, temples, public buildings and tombs, and yielded examples of sculpture, wall painting, pottery, domestic equipment and tools. They led to the discovery of some ten or more temples dedicated to a variety of gods: a Christian church and a synagogue (both built at the end of the 2nd century A.D.), temples of the ancient Babylonian divinities Bel, Shamash and Nanaia, and shrines dedicated to Mesopotamian, Syrian and Palmyrene gods (Aphlad, Hadad, Atargatis, Baalshamash and Aglibol). The soldiers of the Roman garrison worshipped Mithra and Jupiter, and one of the most important temples was that dedicated to Zeus. A great medley of languages was spoken in Dura-Europos: it was a meeting-place for caravans from all the eastern provinces, and the archaeologists found a whole collection of written documents—inscribed sherds, graffiti and parchments—in the Syrian, Palmyrene, Greek and Iranian languages.

The discoveries at Dura-Europos were soon supplemented by the investigation of the Mesopotamian cities of Assur (the results of which were published in 1933—W. Andrae and H. Lenzen, *Die Partherstadt Assur*) and Hatra, a Parthian foundation where excavation had been begun by Andrae at the beginning of the century, but where particular progress was made in the years 1951 to 1954 under the direction of Iraqi archaeologists. The excavations at Hatra have revealed ten temples, a palace, dwelling houses and an amphitheatre. Of particular interest are the magnificent statues of gods and local kings discovered quite recently by the Iraqi archaeologists and dated to the 2nd century A.D. *(Plates 8, 9, 10, 12, 14).*

This work, together with the results of work at Palmyra, Nimrud Dagh and elsewhere, has made it possible to study the culture and historical development of Mesopotamia in the Hellenistic period and has revealed the culture of the most westerly districts of Iran in this period.

Merv and Nisa

In 1930 the Soviet archaeologist A. A. Marushchenko started digging at the ancient inhabited sites of Old and New Nisa, some 12 miles north of the town of Ashkhabad. This was the first step in the archaeological investigation of the original home of the Parthian dynasty. In 1946 systematic excavation was begun at these sites by a large archaeological expedition under the leadership of Professor M. E. Masson; and these excavations, along with the excavations at Old Merv, one of the most ancient cities of the East, are still continuing.

To the Seleucid period in Merv belongs the so-called "wall of Antiochus", built on the orders of Antiochus I to protect the oasis of Merv. It has a total circuit of some 140 miles (1500 stadia).

Round the ancient nucleus of Merv Antiochus erected a new city, called in his honour Antiochia, surrounded by massive walls. Professor Masson's expedition excavated dwelling houses and industrial quarters of this period on the site known as Gyaur-Kala, the palace-fortress of the king's viceroy at Erk-Kala, and remains of the mansions of the nobility. We now know something of the life of the city; the excavators were able to show, for example, that in the industrial quarters of the Hellenistic city, as in the towns of the early Middle Age, the craftsmen in each trade lived in the same district (the districts of the metalworkers and the millers in particular having been identified). The general layout of the town is also clear: like all the Parthian cities known to us, it consisted of the viceroy's citadel, a circuit of walls and towers, densely built-up dwelling areas, and an industrial suburb. The excavations have also revealed the techniques of fortification and the disposition of the gates and towers, and have yielded much evidence on the economy and life of the city.

Still more interesting are the excavations at Nisa. These have shown that Parthian Nisa consisted of three main parts—a citadel covering more

14

18

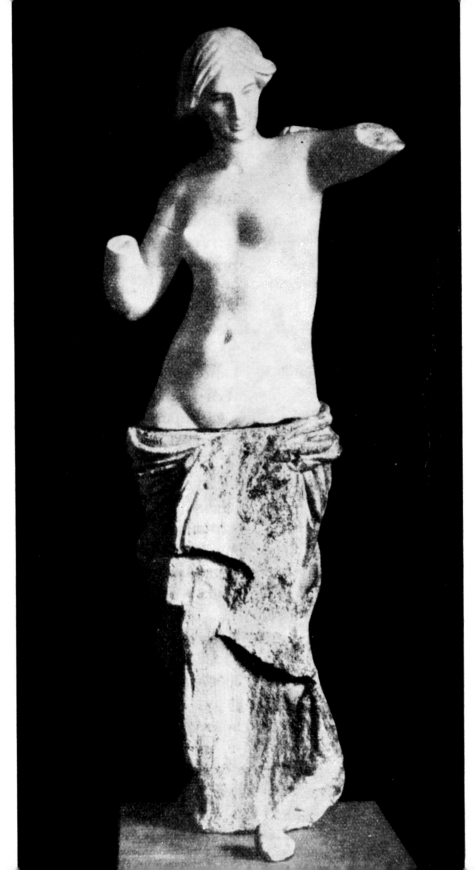

← 24, 25

26

30

than 10 acres, pentagonal in plan, built on a natural crag; the town proper; and the urban precinct surrounded by a defensive wall. Near the town was the fortress of Mihrdatkart, the "royal city" with the burial-place and the treasury of the Parthian kings. In the city were temples dedicated to the cult of ancestors. One of the buildings excavated—the so-called "square room", each side being some 65 feet long—was probably such a temple. In the upper part of its walls were niches containing clay statues of Parthian kings and gods, the ceiling was supported by columns with elaborate capitals, and the hall was decorated with terracotta friezes with a pattern of acanthus leaves, Hercules' club, and lions' heads. In form and colouring the statues found in the hall conformed to the ancient canons. Also at Nisa (in the "square hall", probably built in the 3rd century B.C., in which grave goods from the tombs of the Parthian kings were accumulated) were found some remarkable marble statues, probably imported from Syria. Particularly interesting is a statue of a goddess wringing out her wet hair—one of the commonest representations of Aphrodite in Hellenistic art *(Plate 20)*.

Of particular importance also are the rhytons—cult vessels made from elephants' tusks—which were also found in the "square hall". They came to light in 1948 at the time of the catastrophic Ashkhabad earthquake; and in spite of the difficulties caused by the earthquake and by the early onset of winter in that year, the archaeologists successfully extracted some 40 rhytons, broken into thousands of fragments. The rhytons—masterpieces of Parthian art—have now been restored and adorn the museums of Tashkent, Moscow and Leningrad. They are horn-shaped vessels, standing some 20 inches high, decorated with protomes of centaurs and griffins, the torso of a naked goddess, etc. Round the neck is a band of masks, along with scenes connected with the cult of Bacchus, and representations of the classical gods and goddesses (Zeus, Hera, Athene, Apollo, etc.). Some of the rhytons are decorated with incrustations of multi-coloured glass, silver and bronze. They are very valuable evidence not only for the study of the art of Parthia, but also on the ideology of the period *(Plates 5, 6, 7)*.

At Nisa, too, the excavators had the good fortune to find the archives of administrative documents relating to the wine store which has already been referred to.

Sites in Afghanistan and Pakistan

The discoveries in Turkmenia were later supplemented by the work of the French Archaeological Delegation in Afghanistan, which excavated a number of settlements and temples of the Hellenistic period (of particular interest being the work of Daniel Schlumberger at Surkh Kotal, a dynastic temple of the Kushan period, and the recent discovery of the splendid Hellenistic city of Ai-Hanum), and the work done in north-western India by Sir John Marshall at Taxila, Roman Ghirshman at Begram, etc.

As a result of all this work there emerged a picture of the character and general pattern of the culture of the Hellenistic period in this area.

Investigations in Persia

Thus our knowledge of the culture of Iran in Hellenistic times is based mainly on archaeological excavation in its western and eastern extremities. Iran proper at this period is for all practical purposes an archaeological vacuum. To fill this vacuum we have only the work by Sir Aurel Stein at Shami which has already been mentioned, the remains of the temple of the goddess Anahita at Kangavar (a podium and remains of columns), the two isolated columns of Hellenistic date at the village of Khurkha (between the towns of Sultanabad and Kum), and the excavations undertaken by Ernst Herzfeld at Kuh-i Khwaja in 1926-1928. Much may be hoped for from Roman Ghirshman's investigation of the Seleucid and Parthian levels of Susa, and much new material can also be looked for from the full publication of the results of the work of the Michigan University expedition at Seleuceia on Tigris (carried out in the thirties under the direction of L. Waterman); but it must nevertheless be admitted that the Hellenistic period in Iran proper has not been adequately investigated. This gives added importance to the study of the common features and the differences between the products of the culture of the Hellenistic period found in the West and the East, and to the study of works of art belonging to this period, such as reliefs, statues and coins *(Plates 1, 11, 16, 20, 22, 23, 25, 26, 27)*. We shall have more to say about these works later.

Sassanian Sites

Rather more attention has been paid to the Sassanian period. The most important results are those achieved by the American expedition under the leadership of J. M. Upton at Kasr-i Abu Nasr near Shiraz (southern Iran; excavations carried out in 1932-1934), Professor A. U. Pope's work at Takht-i Sulaiman (southern Azerbaijan), which was continued between 1959 and 1965 by the German Archaeological Institute under the direction of H. H. von der Osten and R. Naumann, and the many years of work at Bishapur and Susa by Professor Ghirshman of the French Archaeological Mission in Iran. Also of interest are André Godard's studies of the Sassanian fire temples, ruins of which have been found in many parts of Iran. These investigations have recently been continued by Professor L. Vanden Berghe, who has also published a valuable general work on the archaeology of ancient Iran *(Archéologie de l'Iran ancien)*.

It is necessary to note also the very promising excavations of a number of Sassanian fortresses in southern Turkmenia which are being carried out by the Institute of History and Archaeology attached to the Academy of Science of the Turkmenian SSR.

The latest in date of the sites mentioned is the small town at Kasr-i Abu Nasr, where the levels which have been excavated belong to the end of the Sassanian period (6th-7th centuries). Here the excavations revealed dwelling houses and commercial and industrial buildings, along with some very interesting tools, pottery, and more than five hundred *bullae* (clay tablets with the impressions of Sassanian seals).

The excavations at Takht-i Sulaiman—the ancient city of Shiz, the sacred place of the Parthians and Sassanians—are not yet complete. A fire temple of very complicated plan and a number of buildings belonging to the palace complex have been discovered, and the fortifications are being investigated. In the 1965 excavation season a sensational discovery was made—over two hundred clay *bullae* similar to those found at Kasr-i Abu Nasr.

Ghirshman's excavations at Bishapur, begun in 1936, have produced results of great importance. In addition to a great quantity of pottery, fragments of stone sculptures and reliefs, and coins, he discovered the remains of the polychrome mosaics which had decorated the floors of the courtyard of the "Large *Iwân*" and the palace. Here too were found the remains of a temple and a very interesting votive monument dedicated to the King of Kings Shapur I, consisting of two columns (one of them with an inscription in Parthian and Middle Persian), the pedestal of a statue, and the remains of stone fire altars.

The other remains belonging to the Sassanian period have so far been studied only sporadically, though they have nevertheless yielded some interesting material—for example the magnificent stucco panels found in the excavations at Damghan and Kish.

Methods of Investigation

The methods of archaeological investigation have been discussed in a number of previous volumes in this series, and the methods applicable to the archaeology of Parthian and Sassanian Iran are similar to those used in the study of the earlier periods of Iran, which were well described in "Persia I". The archaeologists use the technique of excavating sites in successive levels, basing their dating on stratigraphical sections. In dealing with sites of the Hellenistic period and the early Middle Age, however, their object is to carry out excavation over the largest possible areas of the ancient cities and strongholds. This special feature is determined by the task which faces the investigators—the study of the towns of these periods, which is perhaps the most important problem in the history of Iran, and one for which there are few other sources of information. Classic examples of the application of this method are the excavations at Nisa in Turkmenia and the investigations at Dura-Europos and Bishapur.

In the dating of archaeological levels, particularly in small exploratory excavations, and also in the excavation of tombs, great significance attaches to what is called the "archaeological complex"—the finding in association in the same level or in the same tomb of a group of objects, including in particular objects which can be given an exact absolute date (mainly coins and written documents, but also pottery of particular shapes and tools and implements of particular types, etc.). Comparisons can then be made between archaeological complexes of earlier and later date from sites in the same area, and the archaeologists, using the method of "typological series" (first introduced into archaeology by Montelius, and described in earlier volumes in this series), are able to identify ever larger groups of objects which, in turn, can be used to date levels found on other sites.

Since pottery is the material found in greatest quantity in any excavation, and since in excavations covering large areas the quantity of this material is so large that it is frequently possible to establish very extensive series of vessels of different shapes and decoration, it is becoming increasingly common to apply the methods of mathematical statistics and information theory to the description of the material.

We do not, however, rely exclusively on archaeological excavation for our knowledge of the culture of Iran in the Hellenistic period and early Middle Age. A considerable contribution is made also by the study of the arts and crafts of these periods, and also of the coins; and studies of this kind have their own specific objectives and their own specific methods.

The principal method employed in the study of such objects is the "typological series". In its application to the remains of material culture it operates in the following way. We begin by considering a number of details in the design of a range of objects, select a series of analogies, and arrange them in a progression according to their degree of similarity. By considering a number of such progressions for details in a range of objects we can arrange the objects in consecutive series. In order to establish which objects in these series are later and which are earlier, it is necessary to find particular details which in certain representations have lost their original meaning. In using the method of the typological series we are, of course, considering only the formal aspect of the objects in question, and have no means of interpreting their subject matter. But the importance of the typological series is precisely that it is almost independent of any interpretation of the "content" of the objects. At the same time it makes a valuable contribution to our understanding of the objects under consideration, since in order to reveal the pattern of development of particular ideas reflected in the designs included in such a series it is sufficient to interpret—with the help of other sources, written or other—only a few, or even a single one, of the links in the chain.

This method is of course of particular importance when the amount of material at our disposal is limited; and this is the situation which faces us in the periods with which we are concerned in this book *(Plates 104–123)*.

The Study of Coins

Among the material remains those most directly connected with political and socio-economic history are coins; and their significance is particularly great in periods about which the written sources tell us little.

In the East, from the time of the Achaemenids onwards, the right to issue coins in particular denominations belonged exclusively to the ruler of the country. Coins were thus a kind of "official proclamation", and were frequently issued as a means of propaganda on behalf of particular political or ideological conceptions. The study of coins, therefore, often yields much more information about a particular period than any of the other sources. They tell us the names and styles of successive rulers of Iran, and as we follow the changes in title and the succession of the various dynasts we can obtain some insight into the vicissitudes of the fierce struggle for the throne. We may consider one example out of the many that could be quoted.

Coins as Dynastic Propaganda: Varahran and Narseh

Shapur, King of Kings of the Sassanid dynasty and conqueror of the Emperor Valerian, died in the year 273 A.D. Sassanian Iran was then at the zenith of its glory. Shapur's three sons had, during his lifetime, been assigned fiefs in different parts of the country. One of them, Hormizd Ardashir, having previously been declared his father's heir, succeeded to the throne, but died within a few months in circumstances which have not been explained. His two brothers, Varahran and Narseh, had equal claims to the throne, but the succession fell to Varahran. His reign was also a short one, and within two years, in 276, the throne descended to his son, who was also called Varahran (Varahran II). Varahran II ruled Iran for seventeen years and was succeeded by his son, again called Varahran. Within a month, however, the throne was taken over by Shapur's son Narseh *(Plates 113, 114, 115, 117)*.

This bare record of successive rulers of Iran, this changing pattern of names, is all that the written sources tell us, and accordingly in studies of Sassanian Iran we find a constantly recurring statement to the effect that "the cause of these frequent changes of ruler has not yet been established."

In 1924 Ernst Herzfeld published the study to which he gave the name of a village in Persian Kurdistan, *Paikuli*. On this site he discovered an almost totally ruined building surrounded by an accumulation of debris, including blocks of stone with carved inscriptions in Parthian and Middle Persian, remains of stucco decoration, and two poorly preserved stucco busts which, by comparison with coins, could be fairly readily recognised as portraits of the King of Kings Narseh. Herzfeld managed, by dint of immense labour, to fit together the pieces of stone with the inscriptions, and although they did not yield a completely connected text it was possible to establish that the inscription (which was in two versions, one in Parthian and the other in Middle Persian) was composed to the directions of Narseh, and that it referred to a war waged by him against the "king of Sacastan" and mentioned the names of many dignitaries, often with titles of great interest. Herzfeld identified, for example, a "Caesar of Rome", a "king of Khorezm (Chorasmia)", a "Kagan of the White Turks", and many other exotic personalities. The hypothesis he propounded was an interesting one: he suggested that the inscription was concerned with Narseh's struggle for the throne of Iran. It was necessary, however, to prove this hypothesis; and here the coins came to his aid.

The coins of the various rulers of Iran had a number of distinctive features. Thus, for example, Varahran I used the rather unusual designation of "King of Kings of Iran, descended from the gods of Ardashir" (the style usually adopted by the Sassanid kings being "King of Kings of Iran, descended from the gods"), referring specifically to the founder of the Sassanid dynasty. His son Varahran II issued coins bearing not only his own portrait but that of his wife and son (whereas the obverse of Sassanian coins normally bore

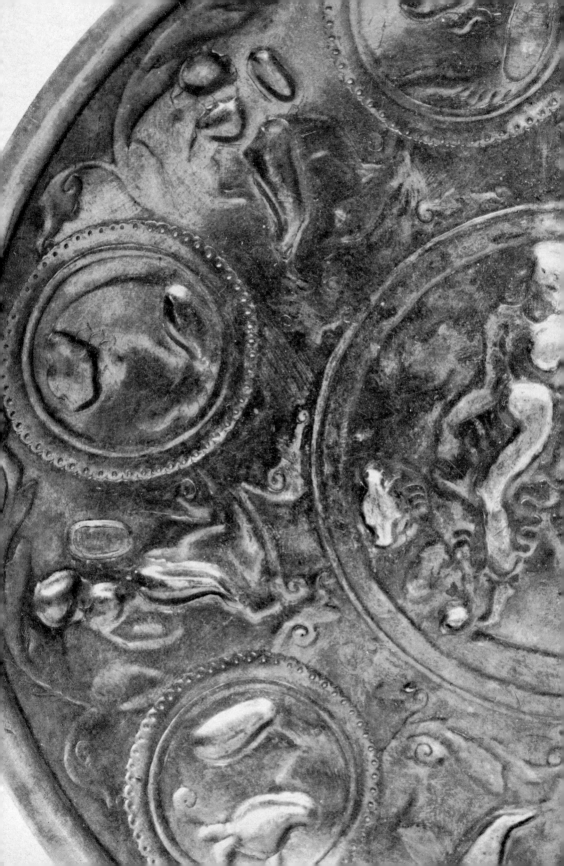

39

38

40   41   42

43

44

45

46

49

52   53   54

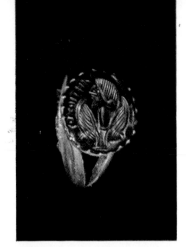

55

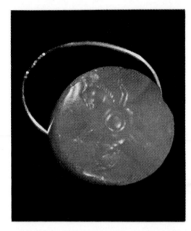

56

57

58

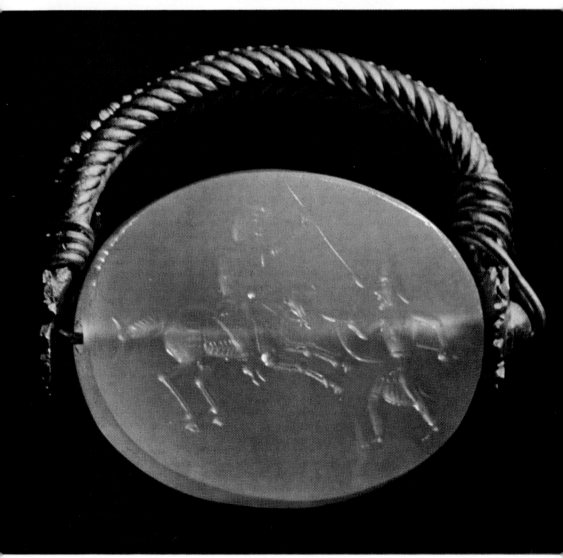

only the head of the King of Kings) *(Plate 113)*. Finally some coins issued by Narseh were found, on which he was represented not with the insignia of power appropriate to him as King of Kings of Iran but in a headdress such as was worn by the rulers of the various provinces—though on these coins he still styled himself King of Iran. Moreover these coins were of gold, and the right of minting gold coins belonged only to the ruler of Iran.

The study of the coins made it possible to bring all the separate facts together in a logical pattern. Varahran's accession to the throne had been preceded by a struggle between different court factions; and on achieving victory in this struggle Varahran sought to proclaim his legitimacy on his coins, appealing for this purpose to the authority of the founder of the dynasty. After Varahran's death his supporters placed his son on the throne of Iran; and again the coins proclaimed the new ruler's claim to lawful authority: in putting the portraits of his wife and son on his coins Varahran II was following the practice already adopted on Roman coins, on which similar portraits were used to establish the direct descent of the throne from father to son. But while Varahran was still on the throne Narseh, at that time ruler of Armenia, began to issue his own gold coins, declaring in this way his title to the throne.

With these facts established, it became possible to make sense of the inscription on the mysterious building at Paikuli. Here Narseh, advancing to the conquest of his father's throne, had been met by his supporters and proclaimed King of Kings of Iran; and the monument—a tower in the form of a tiered altar, decorated with sculptured portraits of the new king—had been erected in honour of the occasion. And this in turn made it possible to interpret certain puzzling passages in other sources. In consequence we have acquired much new and unexpected knowledge. We know something of the life and activities of the chief priest of Iran, Kartir, who was the leader of Varahran's party, and we know the aims of this court clique which sought to transform Iran into a theocratic state and to put all political power into the hands of the priests. We also know who were Narseh's supporters. They did not, it is true, include the "Caesar of Rome" or the King of Khorezm, but they turn out to be the rulers of the western provinces and cities whose rise in the reign of Narseh provides an explanation for much of the later political history of Iran.

A simple explanation was also found for a fact which had hitherto puzzled scholars. In the area round Persepolis, the national shrine of the Persians, all the early Sassanid kings had carved reliefs on rocks representing the scene of the "divine investiture", in which the supreme god of Iran, Ahura Mazda, was shown presenting the King of Kings with the insignia of power. Varahran I had, like the others, caused a representation of his investiture to be carved on the rock. It was easy to recognise the King of Kings represented in each of these carvings, since each Sassanid ruler wore a crown of a particular design, which was not repeated by his successors. On the relief representing Varahran I, however, were carved the name and titles of Narseh. On achieving supreme power in Iran Narseh had clearly used this means of proclaiming the legitimacy of his claim to the throne and of destroying the memory of his predecessor. Thus the study of the coins, by bringing a series of isolated facts into a connected pattern, has opened up a new page in the history of Iran.

Coins and Chronology: the Problem of the Kushans
In the study of coins it is sometimes difficult to know in advance what information can be extracted from them. To a great extent this depends on the method of investigation. Recently much has been learned from the chronological arrangement of the various series of coins according to the punches from which they were struck. Each punch was used to produce considerable numbers of coins, and it is relatively easy to identify the minute peculiarities of each punch (for example, an error in engraving the inscription or a particular method of treatment of some detail). Given the imperfect coining techniques then in use, the punch wore out fairly

quickly and was replaced by a new one. Two punches were used, one with the design for the obverse, the other for the reverse. The two punches did not, of course, wear out at the same rate, and we sometimes find coins stamped on the obverse with an old punch and on the reverse with a new one. Thus, ideally, we could get the following series: coins struck from a given pair of punches; coins using the same punch on the obverse and a new one on the reverse; and coins using a new punch on the obverse and the previous one on the reverse. A series of this kind shows the logical development of the coining process. By using this method we can determine which coins were issued by a particular ruler at the beginning, in the middle and at the end of his reign, and sometimes also the order of succession of different rulers. Since changes in the king's style and titles and in his patron divinities (which were usually represented on the reverse side of the coins of this period) are found relatively frequently in the Hellenistic period and early Middle Age, we can employ the method of chronological arrangement of coins according to the punches used in order to obtain extremely valuable information about the politics or religion of particular periods.

Sometimes a relative chronology established in this way is the only basis we have on which to erect all our historical framework. The most characteristic example of this is offered by the gold coins of the Kushans (*Plates 49, 50*).

The Kingdom of the Great Kushans occupied territory in Central Asia, Afghanistan, Pakistan and northern India. Founded by nomadic tribes (the Yueh-chi, as they are known in the Chinese chronicles), this was one of the most important powers in the late Hellenistic period. Its history and the remarkable achievements of its culture will be discussed in detail in the volumes in this series concerned with Central Asia and India. Here it is necessary only to mention that in the reign of a ruler belonging to the dynasty of the Great Kushans named Kanishka was held the famous

Buddhist council which developed the doctrine of the "Great Vehicle" (Mahayana), the main school of Buddhism, which later spread throughout the whole of Asia and made Buddhism a world religion. In the Kushan period were created the world-famous monuments of Gandhara and Mathura, the basis on which the national art of India developed.

The history of the Kushan kingdom is a landmark of great importance in the story of the whole of the Near and Middle East. Many scholarly works have been written about the Kushans, but hitherto one of the unsolved problems has been that of the absolute chronology of the period, the exact dating of the Kushan kingdom. The difficulty is that the written sources enable us to determine its dating only very approximately (in the early centuries A.D.), and are in any case very few in number; moreover the coins bear no dates, and although we have a number of dated inscriptions the dates are based on an era which is unknown to us or are reckoned from the beginning of the reign of the Kushan ruler Kanishka, which we are unable to relate to any dates known to us. This is the basis of the "problem of the Kanishka era"; and scholars, using all available sources, have sought to find the starting point of the era and so determine the dating of the Kushan kingdom. Among the dates proposed as the beginning of the "Kanishka era" are 78 A.D.; 102 A.D.; 144 A.D.; about 200 A.D.; about 230 A.D.; and 278 A.D. It will be seen that the various hypotheses cover a range of two centuries.

This divergence is a matter of great significance, for example, in the archaeology of Central Asia, Afghanistan and eastern Iran, where the archaeological levels are dated mainly from the Kushan coins found in them. So long, therefore, as we cannot establish absolute dates for these coins we are unable to follow the development of the cultures of vast areas of the Middle East.

The problem of the "Kanishka era" is still unsolved. Here I shall try only to indicate one of the possible approaches to its solution—the typological study of coins.

As a first step let us consider the material which can be fairly exactly dated, the so-called "Kushano-Sassanian" coins—the coins issued by Sassanid rulers after the Sassanids had destroyed the Kingdom of the Great Kushans. Typological analysis makes it possible to demonstrate that the first Kushano-Sassanian gold coins replace the gold coins of the Kushan king after a very short gap of scarcely more than a decade. The Sassanid ruler retained the same design on the obverse, which, as in the last Kushan coins, shows the king wearing the dress and headdress and holding the attributes of the Kushan king. The representation on the reverse, too, is the same as on the last Kushan coins—Shiva and a bull. The lettering of the inscription can be read: it is written in the Greek alphabet adapted for the Bactrian language (the language of the Kushan kingdom)—the alphabet also used for rendering words in the Middle Persian language. The name of the ruler who issued the first Kushano-Sassanian coins was Hormizd.

We are fairly well informed about the history of the Sassanid kingdom, and yet we are unable to determine exactly when these coins were issued. Even though we know that the Sassanid Shahanshah became ruler of the territory of the Kushans (and the regnal dates of all the Sassanid kings are exactly established) and that the Kushano-Sassanian coins were issued in his name, the problem is still unsolved; for in the 3rd and 4th centuries A.D. (the period when the conquest of the Kushan kingdom must have taken place) Iran was ruled by two Hormizds, one in the year 273, the other from 302 to 309. As a result there are two schools of thought. One (led by Ernst Herzfeld) considers that all Kushano-Sassanian coins are to be dated to the 3rd century; the other (represented by A. Cunningham, R. Ghirshman, R. Göbl and others) refers them to the 4th. But we must remember that the ruler of Kushan territory may not have been the King of Kings himself, but perhaps one of his sons. In that event it seems almost impossible to establish the date *(Plates 118, 147)*.

The problem can, however, be solved with the help of the coins. The Sassanid rulers of Kushan territory issued two series of coins simultaneously—one (in gold) on the model of the late Kushan coins, and the other (in bronze and silver) on the model of their own Sassanian coins and bearing legends in Middle Persian. This latter series can be compared with the coins issued for Iran itself. We can establish, for example, that the mint of the city of Merv produced both Kushano-Sassanian coins in bronze and silver and Sassanian silver and gold coins. The typological analysis of both series enables us to determine the succession of the Sassanid rulers of Kushan territory, and sometimes to decide who these rulers were. It has been shown in consequence that the first Kushano-Sassanian coins— minted only in bronze—were issued by the King of Kings of Iran, Shapur II (309-379 A.D.).

The issue of these coins was connected with the start of the Sassanian conquests in the East. From other sources we can establish that these conquests began in the sixties of the 4th century. The next ruler, who issued silver as well as bronze coins of Kushano-Sassanian type, but still following Sassanian models, was Ardashir II (379-383). The typological analysis of copper and bronze coins has made it possible to determine that the next ruler of the former Kushan territory was Hormizd, and we know from other sources that this Hormizd was the son of Ardashir II. He did not, however, reign over Iran: when his father became King of Kings (in the year 379) Hormizd replaced him on the throne of the former Kushan kingdom, and it was this Hormizd who issued the first Kushano-Sassanian gold coins, following very closely the type of the late Kushan coins. It is probable that the issue of the first gold coins marks the final conquest of Kushan territory by the Sassanids; and on this basis the first Kushano-Sassanian gold coins can be dated about the year 379 A.D.

The last ruler of the dynasty of the Great Kushans who is referred to in inscriptions of the Kushan period is Vasudeva, who was on the throne in the 98th year of the "Kanishka era"; and we find this very name on the coins of the late Kushan period from which the first Kushano-Sassanian gold coinage was copied. It would seem, therefore, that the problem of the dating of Kanishka (and therefore of the absolute dating of the Kushan kingdom) is solved: the 98th year of the Kanishka era must be put at the end of the seventies of the 4th century. Can we be sure, however, that the Vasudeva mentioned in the inscriptions and the Vasudeva who issued the last Kushan coins are one and the same? May there not have been two or even three rulers with the same name? This is the view held by some numismatists; for we now possess a considerable quantity of Kushan gold coins bearing the name Vasudeva, and these coins are of very varied types and may have been issued by different rulers. The solution must therefore be looked for by determining the chronological order of coins bearing the name Vasudeva *(Plate 50)*. Only this method can provide a reliable answer to the question whether these coins are to be attributed to a single ruler or to a number of different rulers—though the results obtained by this method would, of course, have to be checked against the other available evidence.

Other Uses of Coins
The examples quoted do not by any means exhaust the types of information which can be obtained from the study of coins. Thus, for example, by establishing the relative chronology of the various types of coin representing different divinities we can obtain a pointer to the religious policy of successive rulers, drawing conclusions from the replacement of the figures or symbols of particular divinities by the figures or symbols of others.

Coins also provide valuable evidence for the attribution of other works of art; for kings and rulers were represented not only on coins but also on rock carvings, seals, metal vessels, and even silk fabrics. We have already noted that each Sassanian ruler wore a crown of characteristic shape; and from the form of the crown we can date any work of art of the Sassanian period bearing the figure of one of the Sassanid kings.

Coins—the most exactly dated evidence we have—also make it possible to establish the form of individual letters of the alphabet typical of a particular period. Palaeographic tables obtained by this method enable us to date other objects bearing inscriptions, but giving neither a date nor the name of any known historical person. The most interesting of such objects are engraved seal-stones; and the study of these seals, engraved in a variety of designs, is one of the main tasks of Iranian studies at the present day.

The Study of Seals

Seal-stones (for which in eastern Iran gem stones were used, with the design engraved in the stone) served as personal seals, and on their miniature surfaces the Iranian artist craftsmen carved the portraits of their owners, the symbols and figures of their patron divinities, and a variety of other devices. The immense value of this branch of art to the archaeologist lies in the great quantities which have been found—comparable only, perhaps, with the massive finds of coins *(Plates 55–103)*.

The range of designs found on the seal-stones is very wide: indeed they show almost all the subjects and themes known to us in works of art of other types. But in contrast, for example, to the designs on vessels made of the precious metals—which are difficult to date with reasonable accuracy—many seals bear inscriptions giving the owner's name or title or some religious formula. By the palaeographical study of such inscriptions—that is, by examining the form of the individual characters—and from the information given by the inscriptions themselves we can date the seals, sometimes within

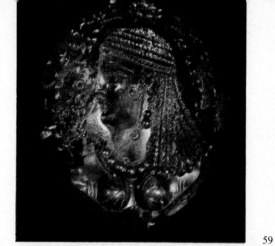

59

60

61, 62 →

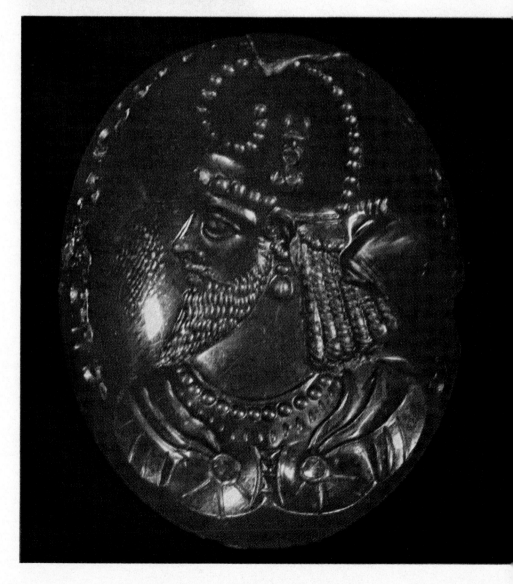

63   64   65
66   67   68
69   70   71

72   73   74

75

76   77   78

79

80

82

83

81

84

85

86

87

88

89

90

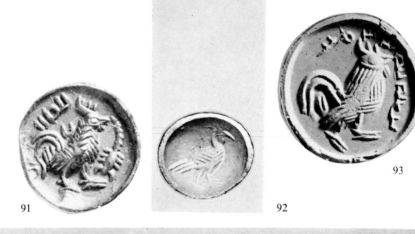

94   91   92   93

95

96

97

98

101

102

103

very narrow limits, and consequently can deduce the time at which particular subjects first appeared or became widely used in the art of Iran.

The "Official Portrait"

As an example of the method we may consider the dating of a group of seal-stones of the early Sassanian period (3rd-4th centuries A.D.) bearing what are known as "official portraits".

In the archaeology of Iran the "official portrait" is a very frequently found theme and one of very great interest. It consists of the figure of a king, high dignitary, official or priest, represented in a rigidly conventional style without any individualised characteristics. In such portraits great stress was laid on the "investitural insignia"—the particular form of headdress, costume, hair arrangement and ornaments which indicated the rank or dignity of the person represented. This type of portrait is found in many branches of art—not only on seals and coins but in rock carvings, works of toreutic art, statues, and so on. Thus a scholar studying this type of subject in a particular art form can draw on a considerable amount of comparative material. But where we are concerned with the dating of objects it is essential to find a "control"—that is, a field in which the dating of a particular subject can be checked against independent data. For the Sassanian period this control is provided by the engraved seal-stones. And in fact by comparing the details of a portrait (the "investitural insignia") with the representation of the same person on such objects as coins (though only when we are considering the investitural insignia of the King of Kings himself, for his portrait alone could appear on the obverse of coins) or carvings (which represent not only the King of Kings but the high dignitaries of his kingdom), by seeking out in the written sources—as it is sometimes possible to do—the names and titles of the personages represented on the seals, and by dating the inscriptions on the seals by palaeographical methods, we can deduce the date of these objects from three different directions, each independent of the other. Thereafter, having established the pattern of development of the investitural insignia and official styles with the help of material dated in this way, we can use the typological method to construct a consecutive series—beginning with the seals and then extending our conclusions to other material. It thus becomes possible to build up a picture of the official hierarchy of the Hellenistic period and early Middle Age as it is recorded in the language of representational art.

The Problem of the Sassanian Bullæ

The study of seals makes a considerable contribution to the solving of a number of historical problems, as the following example will illustrate.

As we have already noted, excavations in Iran have yielded large numbers of *bullae*—clay tablets with the impressions of Sassanian seals. Over 500 of these were found in a small room in the stronghold of Kasr-i Abu Nasr, near Shiraz, which had been destroyed by fire; over 200 in a small room in the temple at Takht-i Sulaiman (Shiz); and another 30 or so in a small room in the Sassanian castle of Ak-Tepe in Turkmenia. Others have occasionally been found in levels belonging to the Sassanian period in Azerbaijan (in the course of excavations at Mingechaur), Georgia and Central Asia. As a rule the *bullae* bear the imprint of a number of seals—sometimes as many as ten or more—often including a seal which consists only of an inscription without any other design. This inscription is in standard form, as follows: "A (giving the name), priest of the town or district of B" *(Plates 95–97)*.

The study of the *bullae* from different parts of Iran revealed a number of significant facts. First, they were all found in small cramped rooms, not at all suited for the preservation of archives; and this suggested that the *bullae* were not used for the sealing of documents. Secondly, the reverse side often preserved the mark of a broad strap or thong to which they were sometimes found attached. This likewise argued against the idea that the *bullae* were used for the sealing of documents. Thirdly, it appeared that the *bullae* found in different parts of Iran—in the south (Shiraz), north-west (Takht-i Sulaiman) and north-east (Ak-Tepe)—bore impressions of the same seals, with the names of the same people, and that the inscriptions giving the name of a priest referred to many different Iranian cities. And finally it was noted that some *bullae* bore two or even three impressions of the same seal.

The connection between these various observations was revealed by the discovery in the written sources of obscure references to the existence of "trading companies" carrying on trade throughout Iran and beyond its frontiers. The *bullae* were probably used to seal the companies' bales of goods, having impressed on them the seals of the members of the company and the official seal of the priest of the place from which the goods were despatched—no doubt as an indication that the bale contained material of good quality and the right quantity and that the traders had paid all necessary dues (for it must be remembered that the whole administration of Sassanian Iran was in the hands of the priests). The *bulla* accompanied the bale of goods, serving as a guarantee of its contents (and we know from the documents that the trading companies carried on a wholesale trade in which it was not the practice to open every bale), and also, after the goods were sold, as an accounting document—the seals impressed on it indicating the share of the profit which each trader was to receive. Thus the study of the Sassanian *bullae* opens up the prospect of important advances in our knowledge of the economy of Iran in the Sassanian period.

Rock Carvings

Information about the hierarchical structure of Iranian society can be obtained from the rock carvings, which were official records designed to commemorate particular events. This is a type of monument which was traditional in Iran and the neighbouring areas and had been known from the most remote antiquity *(Plates 124–134)*.

The Persian rock carvings of the Hellenistic period and early Middle Age have long been known, and yet they are still the source to which scholars constantly return when some new historical fact has been interpreted, some new inscription has been read, some new archaeological evidence has been discovered or understood. They provide a kind of standard against which the correctness of any new theory can be measured. This is because the carvings were directed to all the subjects of the King of Kings, to "the whole world", and were intended to make known the glorious achievements of the King of Kings, his victories over his enemies, his gods and his noble ancestors. In accordance with a very ancient Eastern tradition they were symbolic. Their symbolism was expressed in the particular disposition of the figures of the king and his enemies, his gods, and the dignitaries of his kingdom; in the fact that the king's victory in battle was often represented as a single-handed contest with his enemy—an encounter which in reality might never have taken place; and in the fact that the sculptors never sought to reproduce the individuality of their models, to contrive a bold perspective effect, to achieve any vitality in the scenes they represented. Their method was rather, by the rhythmic repetition of, for example, lines of warriors of completely identical appearance, wearing identical clothes and standing in identical poses (usually with the head in profile, the body facing the front and the legs in profile), to convey as forcefully as possible the strength of the royal guard. In representations of dignitaries of the court or the king's noble ancestors attention was concentrated on their relationship to the king or on their investitural insignia *(Plates 125, 128)*.

Many carvings are of a narrative character—again a very ancient Eastern tradition. The events which they record are represented as taking place in a definite order; exceptionally, they show a single incident. When the Sassanid Shahanshah Shapur I ordered his victory over the Roman Emperor Valerian to be recorded on the rock face at Bishapur (southern Iran), the sculptors represented his three victories in a single carving. Under the hooves of Shapur's horse they showed the Emperor Gordian III, who was killed in the war of 242-243 A.D.; in front of him is the kneeling figure of the Emperor Philip the Arab (whose defeat in one of Shapur's campaigns had been followed by the exaction of a huge war tribute from Rome); and by his side stands the figure of the Emperor Valerian, whom he had taken prisoner during the war of 260. The carving also shows the Shahanshah's guard—a large body of warriors, absolutely identical in appearance and distinguished only by the different types of helmets worn by different regiments—and representatives of the various Roman provinces, distinguished from one another by their dress and ethnic type, and by the objects which they are presenting to the King of Kings by way of tribute.

In 1936 an archaeological expedition from Chicago University working near Persepolis discovered on the plinth of an Achaemenian temple (the so-called "Kaaba of Zoroaster", discussed on page 173 of *"Persia I"*, which was used during the Sassanian period as the temple of the fertility goddess Anahita) a long inscription by Shapur I in three languages—Greek, Parthian and Middle Persian. In this inscription Shapur gives a detailed account of his three wars with Rome, enumerating the provinces he had captured and recording the amount of tribute, the strength of the armies, and so on; and the accompanying carvings represent the principal events of all three wars *(Plate 132)*.

The carvings thus not only illustrated historical events, not only proclaimed the greatness of the King of Kings and his religion, but also expressed—sometimes by a transparent symbolism—particular political and ideological conceptions. In a series of carvings and sculptures at Nimrud Dagh the King of Commagene, Mithridates Callinicus, and his son Antiochus (lst century A.D.) set out their dynasty's claim to descent from the Achaemenid King Darius, presenting their own "official portraits" in scenes of investiture in which they are shown being crowned by their noble Persian ancestors and by Hellenistic divinities *(Plate 29)*. In 1963 appeared a magnificent work by Friedrich Karl Dörner and Theresa Goell *(Arsameia am Nymphaios*, Berlin, 1963) recording the results of archaeological investigations at Nimrud Dagh between 1953 and 1956, in which these carvings and statues, along with numerous inscriptions and other archaeological material, are subjected to the most meticulous examination.

Still more transparent is the symbolism in the investitural carving of Ardashir I, founder of the Sassanid dynasty, at Naqsh-i Rustam (southern Iran). The Shahanshah is shown seated on a horse which is trampling with its hooves the prostrate figure of the last king of the Parthian dynasty, Artabanus V. The supreme god of Zoroastrianism, Ahura Mazda, also shown on horseback, is offering Ardashir a ring, the symbol of royal power. Under the hooves of Ahura Mazda's horse is the figure of the god of darkness, Ahriman. Ardashir's victory over the last Parthian king is thus compared with the victory of the god of light over the god of darkness, and Ardashir's authority is consecrated by the supreme Zoroastrian divinity *(Plate 127)*.

The rock carvings of the Sassanian period are particularly numerous and interesting. Most of them are found in southern Iran, near the ancient national shrine of the Persians; some of them on the very cliffs in which the tombs of the Achaemenid kings are hewn.

Toreutic Art

An important part is also played in the archaeology of Iran by the study of works of toreutic art—vessels of silver, gold and bronze embossed with a great variety of scenes *(Plates 30–48, 135–217)*. This is perhaps the most difficult field to study, since on the one hand these works show clear traces of the influences exerted by different schools and styles, and on the other the craftsmen were particularly steadfast in their attachment to the ancient traditions of metalworking.

The amount of material available is continually increasing, but it is discovered, as a rule, not by archaeologists but by the local peasants in the course of casual digging. Thus, for example, a great hoard was found in the middle of the 1920s at Nihavend in the territory of ancient Media. This consisted of precious vessels and gold ornaments, and was given the name of the "Karen Treasure" after the noble Parthian family of the Karens.

In 1912 shepherds near Poltava (southern Ukraine) stumbled by accident on a hoard which is probably one of the most important ever found in Europe for the quantity and weight of the objects it contained. They included Persian (Sassanian) and Byzantine gold and silver vessels and numerous pieces of gold harness and armour. The archaeologists subsequently established that it was not in fact a hoard but the tomb of some rich Avar prince *(Plate 139)*.

In the 1940s peasants in northern Iran found a metal box containing a number of silver vessels of the Sassanian period and a remarkable Sassanian silk fabric bearing portraits of the Sassanid kings. In recent years unusually large numbers of works of toreutic art have come on to the market. Many of them are said to have come from the tombs of Sassanian rulers somewhere on the southern shores of the Caspian. These vessels are eagerly sought after by museums and private collectors, and some of them, when published, have raised doubts about their genuineness in the minds of the specialists. In consequence the task of scholars concerned with the study of toreutic art has been considerably complicated.

The largest collection of Oriental toreutic art is in the Hermitage Museum in Leningrad. The objects in this collection were found at various times

111

within the territory of the Soviet Union—in the western Urals, the River Kama region, Siberia and Ukraine. Some of them formed part of various hoards (which included not only vessels but also a variety of silver ornaments and coins); others came from ancient local shrines of the northern tribes, having travelled there in the way of trade at a very remote period. The illustrations of toreutic work in this book are mainly from the Hermitage collection.

104

105

106

107

109

108

110   111   112

113

115

116

117

118

120

119

123   122

124 125

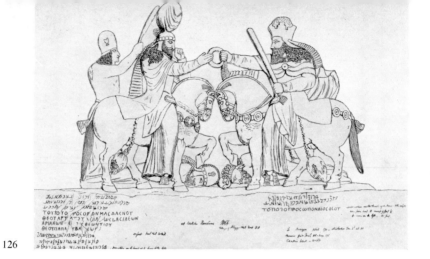

Bm veldig in the Esp side. I the great hun ext. That is Sorta. had termination 127 Mm

PROSPECTS FOR THE FUTURE

III

In this account of the archaeological study of Iran in the Hellenistic period and early Middle Age, and of the methods used by contemporary archaeologists, I have tried to direct the reader's attention to the self-evident fact that the archaeology of Iran in these periods is a complex discipline, and that the study of archaeological material is inconceivable without reference to a wide variety of sources, ranging from historical, literary and religious works by ancient authors and the study of epigraphy to the expert analysis of works of art. The complexity of this approach reflects the complexity of the problems facing the investigator. For these periods, in fact, it would be more accurate to talk of the history of culture rather than of archaeology, for there can be no archaeological study of Iran without taking account of linguistics and philology, numismatics, the history of architecture, and so on.

Thus the problems with which scholars are concerned touch every aspect of the civilisation of these periods: political history, where some of the problems are being successfully solved by the study of the remains of material culture, for example the coins; socio-economic history and the history of the towns, where the solution to the problems is usually to be sought by archaeological excavation; and the history of religion, where the problems are closely connected with the study not only of the temples which have been excavated and the sculptures and frescoes which have been discovered by the archaeologists but also of a wide range of works of art.

It is not possible in this work even to enumerate all the problems with which the archaeology of Iran has to deal. In the following pages I shall attempt to give some account of only a few of these problems—those which seem to me most interesting or with which I am myself concerned. Some of the problems have already been discussed in earlier chapters.

The Pattern of Hellenistic Civilisation

In the first place it is necessary to define what we mean by Hellenistic civilisation. The term is applied to the very distinctive social and political structure and the very distinctive culture which developed in the East in the period following Alexander's conquests. Thereafter the culture of the East retained its Hellenistic imprint for more than five hundred years.

At the time of the establishment of the Seleucid monarchy there was a conflict in the East not only between two cultures, the Hellenic and the Oriental, but also between two ideologies, that of the free citizens of the *polis* and that of the subjects of the Oriental despots. The process was one of interpenetration. The effort of the Seleucid monarchs to create unity out of a motley pattern of different social conditions, beliefs and customs, which was made possible mainly by the process of urbanisation, was—as we have already noted—facilitated by the fact that when the Greco-Macedonians arrived in the East they found a basically similar social structure and similar political conceptions in existence there. For a considerable period, therefore, the predominant ideology was a form of cosmopolitanism, a kind of cultural and political *koiné*. The Parthian kings issued coins based on Greek models, and referred to themselves in their official styles as "Philhellenes"; and the Parthian King Artabanus III wrote a letter in Greek to the Persian city of Susa, modelling himself exactly on Seleucid administrative practice. The two parchments from Avroman and "Parchment No. X" from Dura-Europos, which have already been discussed, were also written in Greek and followed Hellenistic legal forms, though none of the people mentioned in these documents were Greek. At the same time the capital cities of the Hellenistic monarchies and towns with a substantial Greek population saw a considerable development of the palace style of architecture—which was unknown to the democratic *polis*—and much building of elaborate temples, in which the part containing the altar was separated from the temple proper and developed into an independent structure (as, for example, in the great altar of Pergamon); and Aramaic was used along with Greek as an official language of the Seleucid empire.

It would seem, therefore, that the process as a whole is clear and comprehensible: in the early Hellenistic period we are concerned with a uniform culture stretching from the Euphrates to the Ganges. This seems, too, to be confirmed by the archaeological evidence; for the coins issued by the rulers of the Greco-Bactrian kingdom which was formed in Central Asia, Afghanistan and northern India about the year 250 B.C. are splendid examples of the Hellenistic coiner's art, and the latest results achieved by the French Archaeological Delegation in Afghanistan, along with Soviet archaeologists, at the township of Ai-Hanum on the banks of the River Pyandzh reveal the culture of a large Hellenic city, many hundreds of miles from the main centres of the Seleucid empire.

In fact, however, the number of Hellenistic cities known in Iran is relatively small. Susa was a *polis*, under the name of Seleuceia on Eulaeus; Nihavend (Laodicea) was a Hellenistic city celebrated for its temple, which was probably dedicated to the deified wife of Antiochus IV; and there is known to have been a Hellenistic city (Alexandria) in the Kirman area. But all these cities lay on the trade route linking Seleuceia with the distant town of Bactra (Balkh). The influence of the Seleucids, which was felt so strongly in Syria, and the influence of Greek culture, which was so marked in the Far East, were much less in evidence in the northern and southern regions of Iran.

The area round Persepolis (the region known as Persis or Fars) was ruled from the middle of the 3rd century B.C. to the 3rd century A.D. by a local dynasty; and although very little material has survived from the period of dominance of this dynasty—mainly coins and two poorly preserved rock carvings—we are able to assert quite definitely that the culture of this area was practically untouched by Hellenistic influence and continued to develop ancient Oriental traditions dating back to the Achaemenian period. Fars is one of the most striking examples of this, but by no means the only one. Thus the task of archaeology is to study the culture of the different regions of Iran in the Hellenistic period, the combination of a uniform *koiné* with the autochthonous development of ancient Oriental traditions in the various regions. For Iran this problem is of great significance, since the post-Hellenistic period—the early Middle Age—appears on the surface to take the form of a sharp reaction against the Hellenistic world, a Renaissance of ancient Oriental cultural and ideological characteristics; and we must, of course, seek to explain the basis of this Renaissance.

The Parthian Contribution

The second problem, which can be solved mainly by archaeological means, is that of establishing the Parthian contribution to the Hellenistic culture of the East. As the reader will recall, the Parthian kingdom was founded by nomadic tribes from Central Asia. We could reasonably expect, therefore, to find the well-known Scytho-Sarmatian style of art and certain other features (for example, the so-called "polychrome style") diffused over the large area covered by the Parthian kingdom; and this would be of particular significance for Iran, since the Parthian period in its history was the first real unification of the country since the Achaemenian period. And we do in fact find this, though in rather unexpected circumstances.

During the Parthian period we can observe certain uniform features throughout the whole expanse of the Parthian empire. We have already noted, for example, the uniform layout of their towns, and we may note also, as a standard feature of their architecture, the structural element known as the *iwân*, a room open on one side with an arched entrance: this feature is found in Assur, a town barely touched by Hellenistic influence, in the

132

strongly Hellenised city of Hatra, and in the homeland of the Parthians, at Nisa and Merv. The Parthian temples, which have not so far been found in Iran but have been excavated at Nisa, Taxila (Punjab), Assur, Hatra and Dura-Europos, are built in a variety of different materials but show a number of common features. They were usually erected on a platform or podium and consisted of a windowless *cella* separated from the external wall by an ambulatory. The entrance to the *cella*, the inmost shrine of the temple, usually took the form of a portico supported by columns. The art of the Parthian period showed a preference for scenes of hunting, banqueting and fighting, the themes which were later to be so characteristic of the art of Iran in the Sassanian period.

It appears, therefore, that in the Parthian period we find a new *koiné* diffused throughout the whole empire. What led to the development of this common culture? Was it merely the fact that the empire was now ruled not by Greeks but by Iranians?

In considering this problem let us take a particular example, the characteristic feature of the art of Parthia in this period known as "frontality". The first appearance of this particular problem can be traced to the publication of Breasted's book, already referred to, *Oriental Forerunners of Byzantine Painting;* that is, to the discovery of the frescoes of Dura-Europos. The most significant examples in this respect are the Conon paintings from the temple of the Palmyrene gods (probably end of lst century A.D.), the Tribune paintings from the same temple (second half of 2nd century A.D.), and the paintings in the *cella* of the temple of Zeus Theos (beginning of lst century A.D.).

In all these works the figures are represented looking straight ahead at the spectator, with no sense of being involved with the other members of the group. Characteristic of the paintings are the absence of all freedom of movement, the rigidity of the attitudes, the monotonous repetitions of the same techniques of foreshortening. The figures are drawn conventionally against a conventional background, almost devoid of detail: the whole life of the scene seems to be concentrated in the fixed stares of the huge eyes gazing straight at the spectator. The pictures are entirely lacking in the liveliness of the Hellenistic period, but there is an immaterial quality about them which seems to create an invisible spiritual bond with the spectator. We find in them the features which are so strikingly evident in, for example, the famous Ravenna mosaics of the early Byzantine period, and are characteristic of the Christian art of Byzantium.

Dura-Europos offers us the most striking examples of frontal composition, but by no means the only ones. In sculpture this form of composition is characteristic of Palmyra and Hatra; among minor plastic works it is found in the group of rhytons from Nisa in the so-called "hieratic style" (probably also dating from the early 1st century A.D.), which show the same characteristics in the treatment of the faces of Hellenistic divinities. These characteristics are also found in the art of Gandhara.

The frontal representation of divinities is undoubtedly an ancient Oriental feature. It was certainly characteristic of the art of northern Mesopotamia as early as the 3rd millennium B.C., and is found in Persia at a much later period (for example, under the Achaemenids). Rostovtzeff suggested that this technique was borrowed from ancient Oriental art by the Medes and was subsequently brought by the Sarmatians (who were also Iranians) to the northern Black Sea coast, and by another branch of the Iranian peoples south-eastwards into Parthyene, from where it spread still farther. There is another school of thought (represented by E. Will: cf., for example, *Le relief cultuel gréco-romain*, Paris, 1955) which sees the starting point in Greek art, from which the frontal method of composition spread to the Hellenistic art of the East *(Plates 5, 6, 7)*.

This fascinating problem seems to me, however, merely a particular aspect of a more general problem, the development of ideas in the Hellenistic period and early Middle Age.

Syncretism and "Universal Religions"

In the 1st century A.D., throughout the whole expanse of the Parthian empire, an interesting phenomenon can be observed. Out of the immense variety of religious cults, teachings and schools there begins gradually to emerge a certain unity: the gods of the most different religions contract, as it were, dynastic marriages, becoming amalgamated with one another and creating a kind of common religious language. In the series of carvings in Commagene which have already been mentioned Mithridates Callinicus and his son Antiochus are represented along with Heracles, who is identified with the Persian god of victory Verethragna; with Zeus, who is seen as the supreme Persian divinity, Ahura Mazda, god of light; and with Apollo, who is shown with the attributes of the Persian sun god Mithra *(Plate 29)*. The cult of the sun god was very widely diffused, under a variety of names— the Semitic gods Baal and Aphlad, the Greek Zeus, the Persian Ahura Mazda and Mithra.

We find the same thing happening with the cult of the god of victory—the Persian Verethragna, the Greek Heracles, the Indian Shiva—and of the mother goddess, called by the Persians Anahita, by the Semites Nanaia or Atargatis, by the Greeks Artemis. This was, of course, the consequence of particular social and economic changes. The rulers of the great world empires of the East sought to achieve a divine parallel to their own far-reaching power in the establishment of these unified divinities, and almost every one of the religious systems of the East began to lay claim to the status of a universal religion. The syncretism, the common religious language which developed in the Hellenistic period was soon superseded by the quest for a uniform dogmatic religion; for the unity of the gods who manifested themselves under a number of different names was very quickly recognised by their worshippers.

Towards the end of the Parthian empire the religious syncretism which had developed during the Hellenistic period provided a basis for the rise and spread of Christianity in the most westerly regions of the empire. On the eastern frontiers of Parthia, in the Kushan kingdom, there grew up at about the same time another world religion—Buddhism. In the economic centre of Parthia there were laid down at the same period the accepted canons of Judaism. And finally there began in southern Iran, in Fars, the process of transforming Zoroastrianism into a uniform state religion. In all this we see general historical processes at work.

Similarly the frontal method of composition which is found on such a large scale in the Parthian art of this period probably represents ideological changes. It expresses the basic idea of the strictly formulated and dogmatic "universal religions", which saw man as wholly dependent on his gods.

Interesting as these generalisations are, however, it seems to me more important to undertake a thorough study of the material remains, which will enable us to follow this process in detail, to appreciate the course of its development and thus to increase our understanding of its significance.

The Problems of Zoroastrianism

Of particular importance in Iran are the problems connected with Zoroastrianism. In their rock carvings the Achaemenid rulers proclaimed the supreme divinity of Zoroastrianism, Ahura Mazda, as their divine patron. Zoroastrianism was also widely diffused throughout the Parthian empire:

138

137

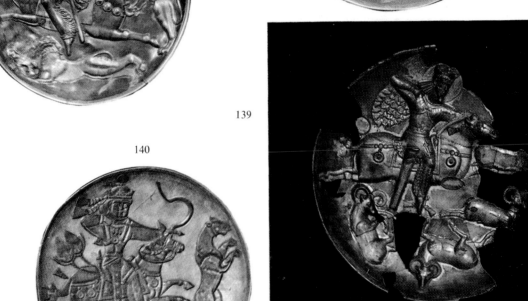

139

140

141

143　　　　　　　142

144

145

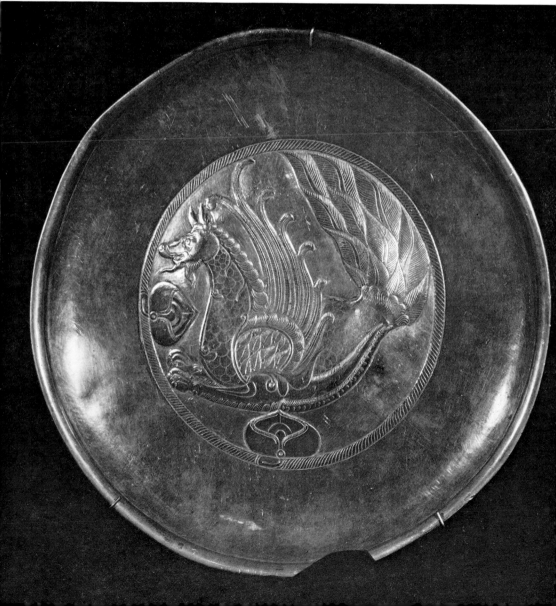

146

147

148

149

154   153

155   156

158

159

161

160

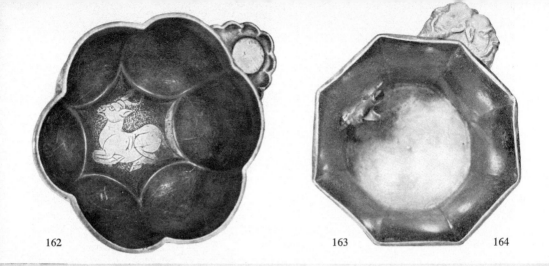

162   163   164

the archives of the wine store of Mihrdatkart, for example, contain more than 400 personal names of officials and place names, the overwhelming majority of which contain the names of the principal Zoroastrian gods— Ahura Mazda, Mithra, Rashnu, Verethragna, and so on.

Later Zoroastrian writings also date to the Parthian period (the reign of one of the Parthian kings named Valarsh or Vologeses) the codification of Zoroastrian doctrine and the production of a written text of the *Avesta*. But this is by no means confirmed by the material remains. In the styles and titles of the Parthian kings, in their representations on coins, and in other evidence there is no reference to the symbols and religious formulae of Zoroastrianism, and although at Mihrdatkart the documents found were dated according to the Zoroastrian calendar and many officials bore Zoroastrian names, the works of art used in the funerary cult of the Parthian rulers were full of typical Hellenistic themes.

The Genesis of Sassanian Art

Within the territory of Iran we know only one area where the old faith was jealously preserved. This was the region of Fars, the country of origin of the Achaemenids and the first domain of the Sassanids. On the coins of the rulers of Fars we find the figure of Ahura Mazda, the fire altar which is the symbol of Zoroastrianism, and a representation of the "Kaaba of Zoroaster", the temple of the Zoroastrian goddess Anahita.

At first sight it looks as if the facts known to us are easily explained: at the time when a religious *koiné* was in existence the right conditions had not developed in the Parthian empire for Zoroastrianism to be declared the state religion, and accordingly the symbols of this religion are not found on official monuments. In the most general sense this can be accepted as accurate, but a detailed study shows the very complicated nature of the process.

For in fact what representations are we expecting to find? It is well known that Zoroastrianism conceived its principal gods Ahura Mazda (the god of goodness and of light) and Ahriman (the god of evil and of darkness) in the form of abstract ideas. The only divinity conceived in anthropomorphic form—if we are to judge from the Zoroastrian religious texts—was Anahita, whose statue is described in the *Aban-Yasht*. And it was probably for this reason that when the artists of Achaemenian Iran sought for the first time to create an image of Ahura Mazda they borrowed a symbol from an alien religion—the god Ashur, represented in the form of a figure on top of a solar disc clad in the insignia of their sovereign, the crenellated crown and the so-called "Persian costume". The adoption of the iconography of alien gods into the Iranian pantheon is a very characteristic feature of Achaemenian art: the Iranian divinity of water, Gopat Shah, for example, was represented also as Shedu, the "guardian of the gates" of the Assyrian palaces *(Plates 57, 74, 75, 77);* and a variety of symbolic representations — such as the fight of a hero with lions or the fight between animals (a lion and a bull, for example)— entered the repertoire of Achaemenian art and were re-interpreted in the light of Zoroastrian ideas. In this way many ancient Oriental features became an organic part of the art of Iran, taking on new interpretations in the process; and accordingly we are probably justified in expecting to find archaic characteristics in works of fairly late date.

We find ourselves faced, however, with a lacuna of more than five hundred years. Between the time of the Achaemenids and the Sassanian period, when many ancient Oriental forms and themes received a fresh lease of life and became perhaps the most fundamental element in the art of Iran, lies the Hellenistic period, during which such forms and themes are practically unknown, or at any rate are found on a very limited scale. The explanation may simply be that in the Sassanian period Zoroastrianism was transformed into a state religion, and that accordingly it was necessary deliberately to resuscitate ancient themes and symbols and to make extensive use of them in the new official art. This explanation is the one most commonly accepted nowadays. The art and culture of Iran in the Sassanian period are seen as a Renaissance of the ancient art of Iran, as a reaction by the national Persian state against the "non-national" art of the Hellenistic period and the "non-national" Parthian rulers of Iran.

Let us, however, consider the material evidence. The earliest works of the Sassanian period do in fact present a sharp contrast to the works of the Hellenistic period. These works are mainly the rock carvings of Fars, the coins of the first Sassanid kings, the colossal stone statue of Shapur I found in a cave in the cliffs, also in Fars, and a small number of gems and works of toreutic art.

What principally strikes us is the limited range of subjects. In the carvings we find only representations of the divine investiture, triumphs or single-handed combats, and the figures of the King of Kings and his court; on engraved gems mainly "official portraits" of the officials and priests of the King of Kings; on toreutic works scenes of hunting, showing the king and high dignitaries, or again their official portraits. This was the pattern of Persian art throughout almost the whole of the 3rd century. We do seem, in fact, to be faced with a Renaissance of ancient Oriental art, manifested in the symbolic and narrative character of the themes, in the stress laid on the divine essence of the royal power, even in the sites selected for the most monumental of the works, the rock carvings, which were hewn in the same cliffs as contained the tombs of the Achaemenid kings. All this does indeed look like a reaction against the heritage of the Hellenistic age.

We have already noted that these works belong to the official art of the Sassanids, and that their function was to give expression to particular political and ideological conceptions on behalf of the new state. But this was not, after all, a particularly new idea of the function of art.

Within the last few years Professor Ghirshman discovered at Susa a carved stone of great interest, the "Stele of Khvasak", which shows a King of

Kings of the Parthian dynasty, Artabanus V, holding out the symbols of power to Khvasak, satrap (governor) of Susa, with an accompanying Parthian inscription. Other monuments of the Parthian period are known—carvings and inscriptions, with figures of the Parthian kings and their governors of the various regions and cities. These carvings and inscriptions were cut to the orders of these high personages, and reflected basically the same ideas as the rock carvings of the Sassanid Shahanshahs. Like them they proclaimed the ideas of legitimacy, like them they showed scenes of investiture; but with this difference that the governors derived their authority over the territories they ruled not from the gods but from the King of Kings of Iran.

In the earliest Sassanian works we are struck by the costume and investitural insignia worn by these dignitaries, but a closer study reveals that they too are identical with the official dress of the late Parthian rulers. We are struck, too, by the rigidity of the figures, the stiffness of their movements, the stress on monumentality, the lack of individuality in the treatment of the figures. Again, however, we find these features in late Parthian art.

Thus all the features characteristic of early Sassanian work already exist in the late Parthian period—with the difference, however, that this style of art is not the only one found in the Parthian empire.

When the Sassanids came to power in Fars, in fact, they erected one of the schools of Parthian art into the style of the whole empire; and they did so with quite definite political and ideological objectives. It is not so much a question, therefore, of a deliberate reaction against the "non-national" art of the Parthians, as of the different character of the Sassanian as compared with the Parthian state, the different nature of its ideology, and the specific conditions of a period when Iran had reached the stage of establishing for the first time a uniform dogmatic state religion and a theocratic form of government.

We must also bear in mind the historical situation of the time. The first Sassanid Shahanshahs—so recently the petty rulers of Fars, a region which jealously preserved the ancient Achaemenian traditions—had set out on a major campaign of conquest in Mesopotamia and had come into contact for the first time with the culture of the late Hellenistic period. The Persian forces who captured Dura-Europos and found there dozens of temples dedicated to many different gods were able to see for themselves that many Palmyrene, Babylonian and Syrian divinities bore Greek and Roman names, and that many Roman gods were no more than Roman versions of Semitic divinities. And the Persian troops who captured Hatra saw very much the same kind of thing—exemplified in the works recently discovered by the archaeologists, a statue of the ancient god Ashur-Bel wearing Roman military uniform, with the goddess Tyche at his feet and a Medusa's head on his cloak *(Plate 10)*, a statue of the local goddess Allat wearing a helmet and holding a spear, in the pose in which Athene was usually represented, a statue of the Persian god Mithra with the eagles which were his symbols *(Plate 12)*, statues of Heracles and Hermes, and even the fire altars with which the Persian soldiers were familiar at home.

Christianity, the infinitely various philosophical doctrines of the Gnostics and the neo-Platonists; the ancient cosmogonic and cosmological ideas of Babylon; Judaism; the cult of the ancient Iranian sun god Mithra, who was an object of particular worship for the soldiers of the Roman garrisons scattered about in military camps from the Euphrates to the Rhine—such was the background, full of contradictions and contrasts, against which the new state grew up. This background was inevitably reflected in the development of Iran: Shapur I, for example, seeking to replace the motley pattern of beliefs by a single uniform faith which should appeal to large numbers of people and be easily comprehensible to all, permitted the propagation of the teachings of Mani—a typical late Hellenistic "universal religion" which accommodated almost every god who was then worshipped. In art this background is perhaps most strikingly reflected in Bishapur, the city built by Shapur I using the labour of Roman prisoners. The excavations carried out here by the expedition led by Professor Ghirshman achieved remarkable results. The most interesting discovery was the mosaics decorating the floor of the reception room of the palace of the King of Kings and the "Large *Iwân*". The mosaics are in the "Syro-Roman" style, and their themes were no doubt imitated from mosaics of the same period, for example in Antioch. The parts which have been preserved contain portraits of actors and theatrical masks, dancing girls, musicians, flowers and fruits. It may well be that the choice of designs for these mosaics, imported by foreign mosaic-workers, was determined by the particular objectives the Persians had in mind: they sought to embellish the reception room with a floor decoration representing one of the most important Zoroastrian festivals—the spring festival of the New Year—and it may be for this reason that their choice fell on the dionysiac themes which were so popular in Mesopotamia. However this may be, it is certain that in the 3rd century the influence of Hellenistic civilisation and its traditions was at first very clearly evident— even in Fars, even in the palace of the King of Kings himself *(Plates 179, 180)*.

Images of Divinity

In the investitural carvings of the Sassanid kings the symbols of authority were presented to the king by Ahura Mazda or Anahita, and in the investitural scenes on the reverse of Sassanian coins the divinities Ahura Mazda, Anahita and Mithra are shown with the Shahanshahs at the fire altars. The first anthropomorphic images of the Zoroastrian divinities are found in the early Sassanian period. We have already noted that a very characteristic feature of the Hellenistic period is the identification of different gods with one another: thus a representation of Heracles might be thought of as Verethragna, or (as at Hatra) Athene might be seen as the local goddess Allat, and might indeed have this name inscribed on the pedestal of the statue. But from the point of view of the representational canon Heracles was portrayed in the accepted Greek style, and the delineation was not dependent on the particular significance read into the figure of the god. In Sassanian art, however, a special canon was established for the representation of the Zoroastrian divinities. But this was in no sense a reversion to the themes and symbols of the Achaemenian period. The figure of Ahura Mazda, for example, repeats the type and the iconographical details of the founder of the Sassanid dynasty, Ardashir I, and the figure of Anahita is scarcely distinguishable from the canonical representation of the Queen of Queens of Iran: the prototypes of the Zoroastrian divinities, in fact, were provided in the Sassanian period by the kings and queens themselves.

In these cases, however, we are dealing only with the supreme divinities of Zoroastrianism: what is the situation with the other gods and goddesses?

We learn from the Zoroastrian sacred texts of the various forms of hypostasis or reincarnation of the Zoroastrian divinities. Thus, for example, according to Zoroastrian mythology the god of victory Verethragna transformed himself successively into a bull, a horse ("beautiful, golden-horned, covered with a golden saddle-cloth"), a camel ("powerful, kicking out with its hooves, clothing people in its shaggy wool"), a wild boar ("charging forward, with sharp teeth, valiant, with sharp tusks"), the bird Varagn ("far seeing", a raven or an eagle). In exactly the same way the divinity of good fortune, Hvarnah, appeared to kings and heroes and to Zarathustra himself in the form of a ram or a bird of prey or a fish or a white horse.

No less numerous are the transformations of the star Tishtrya (Sirius, the benevolent god of Zoroastrianism), the god Mithra, and other divinities. It may well be, therefore, that the profuse ornamentation which is so characteristic of Sassanian art was made up of symbols of the various divinities. And we may go on to ask how this feature made its way into the art of the Sassanids.

In 1886 a hoard of silver vessels was found at the village of Nizhne-Shakhorovka, near Perm. Among the vessels was a magnificent silver cup decorated with an elaborate design. In a roundel in the centre was the figure of a naked goddess with a lion, in medallions round the central group were protomes of various animals (a humped ox, a bear, a horse, a lion and a wild boar), in between the medallions were figures of gladiators with shields, swords and spears, and the blank spaces were filled in with vegetation and palmettes. This vessel long puzzled scholars. Various dates were suggested for it, ranging from the 3rd century B.C. to the 13th century A.D., and various provenances ranging from Syria to Bactria. It provided an excellent example of the difficulties which face scholars in seeking to interpret works of toreutic art.

The discovery of further material, however, offered the prospect of dating the cup more exactly. The details of the decoration, the proportions of the parts, the design of the medallions, the style and technique proved to be identical with those of two early examples of Sassanian toreutic work—a silver kylix discovered at Sargveshi (Georgia), bearing portraits of the Sassanid Shahanshah Varahran II along with his wife and heir, and a dish found at Krasnaya Polyana (Abkhazia) showing a Sassanid prince engaged in a boar-hunt. The dish from Nizhne-Shakhorovka was then shown to have been made in the early Sassanian period, and it thus became easier to identify its prototypes. The central medallion was seen to contain a rather clumsy representation of the goddess Cybele with a lion, a very frequent theme in Roman art, and the surrounding groups could be recognised as fights between gladiators and wild beasts, also a common theme in Roman art. These themes, however, had clearly been re-interpreted by the artist in his own fashion: the protomes of animals were enclosed in the medallions just as the official portraits of the king, queen and prince on the kylix from Sargveshi were framed in medallions and surrounded by typical Roman ornament; the figures of gladiators were transformed into a mere background decoration; and the whole composition—so logically organised in Roman works of art— was destroyed.

168   167

169

170

171

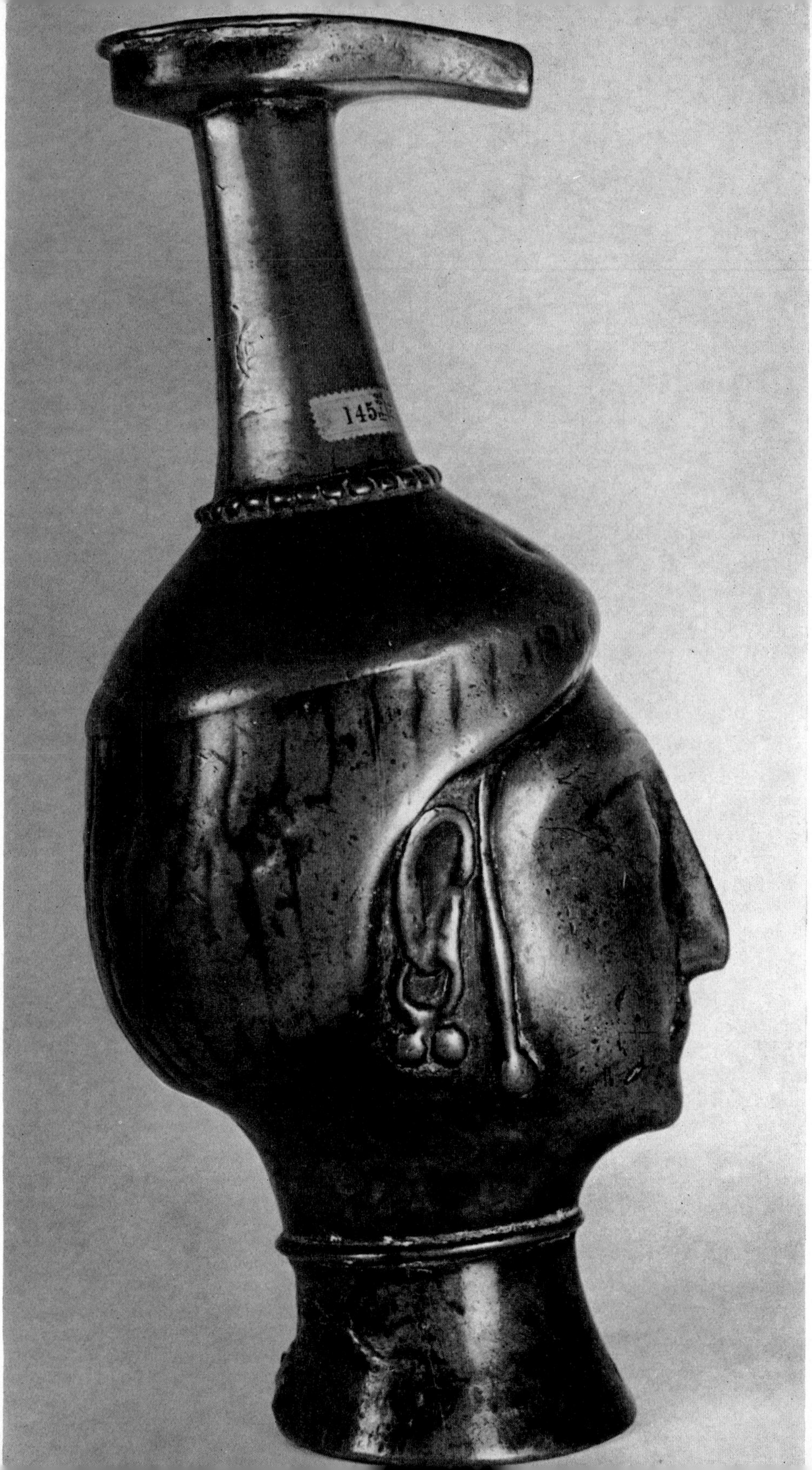

172

173

174

177   175   176

178

180   179

185, 186, 187 →

182

183

184

188   189   190

191

192 193

Of interest also were the protomes of animals used on the dish—the humped ox, the wild boar, the horse and the lion. These are the very incarnations of Zoroastrian divinities which were later to become so popular in Sassanian art. Accordingly the subject of the dish was seen to be typically Zoroastrian. The figure in the centre was evidently the goddess Anahita, and the surrounding medallions contained incarnations of the gods Verethragna (the wild boar), Tishtrya (the horse), Mithra (the lion) and the "primal ox" (the humped ox). This is perhaps the first appearance in Sassanian art of animals as symbols of Zoroastrian divinities; but the origin of these representations is to be found not in reminiscences of ancient Oriental art but in Hellenistic and Roman prototypes. In other words the explanation is to be sought not in a deliberate reaction against Hellenistic culture but in the readiness of Zoroastrianism to adopt alien iconographic formulae to represent its divinities. In this example we are close to the sources of all Sassanian art. If we had only the single work which we have been considering it would be difficult to be confident about the conclusions we have drawn from it; but fortunately this is not so. At about the same time as the dish from Nizhne-Shakhorovka was made the same themes were beginning to appear on those typical products of official Sassanian art, the coins. On the coins of Varahran II the headdresses of the Queen of Queens and the heir to the throne are crowned with protomes of a wild boar, a lion, a horse, a bird, and the sacred dog-headed bird of the Zoroastrian religious texts, the Senmurw. At about the same time, too, we find representations of the humped ox, the lion, the winged horse and other animals becoming increasingly common in Sassanian glyptic art. And this is followed by the appearance of the same themes in other art forms—stucco decoration, silver and gold vessels and fabrics.

Thus the representations of animals as symbols of the Zoroastrian divinities which occur for the first time in the middle of the 3rd century become a regular theme of all Persian art. In these representations the whole resources of the art of the period are deployed: amidst the Sassanian ornamentation we come across features for which analogies can be found in the art of the

Parthian period (for example the figures of animals on late Parthian coins) in the art of Rome and in ancient Oriental art (for example the figure of Gopat Shah, which can scarcely be distinguished from the representations found in the Achaemenian period, the theme of the fight between a lion and a bull, which goes back to a still earlier period, or the dionysiac themes so popular in Roman art) *(Plates 190, 215)*. Here again, therefore, we are concerned not with a deliberate Renaissance but with a natural process *(Plates 72–84, 144, 145, 152, 156, 158, 159, 165–170, 194–197, 200, 202, 206, 208–210)*.

If we study the subjects represented on gems—the material which has survived in greatest quantity from Sassanian times and shows the greatest variety of subject—we note the occurrence of the same themes on the most varied objects. Thus we find engraved on gems the official portraits of high dignitaries and great lords, scenes of the imperial investiture, fantastic creatures like griffins *(Plates 73, 76)*, and the same varied range of animals as are represented on works of toreutic art and in stucco.

The very fact that these subjects occur in such a wide variety of works of ths Sassanian period raises the question of the importance of established canoni and symbolism in this art. But although the Sassanian engraved gems constltute our largest body of evidence, the total quantity of themes is still not large. A few thousand gems, with a few dozen different themes, probably represent the full range of subject matter of Sassanian art. But nevertheless we may suppose that in this field also a similar process took place to that which we observed in the Sassanian official portrait. The symbolic representations of various Zoroastrian divinities developed into the art of the whole empire, the official art of the Sassanid court.

The Hellenistic ideology of Iran was now superseded by the ideology of the centralised state; the religious *koiné* was superseded by a uniform state religion; and the art of the Hellenistic cities gave place to the art of the Sassanid court.

We cannot, however, leave the matter there. If we study the appearance and disappearance of the various symbols we may perhaps be able to follow the development of Zoroastrianism and the emergence of different trends in the ideology of Iran in this period. I should like to conclude this book with a brief discussion of a most interesting personality in early Sassanian history, Kartir, chief priest of Iran *(Plate 124)*. My aim will be to show how the various written sources and the material evidence now available make it possible to gain an entirely new insight into the history of the whole period.

Ideology and Politics

Near the famous edict by Shapur I recording his victories over Rome which was discovered by an expedition from the Chicago Institute in 1936 was found a long inscription by the chief priest, Kartir, written in Middle Persian. Before this discovery three inscriptions written to his instructions were already known. One was at Naqsh-i Rustam, beside the carving representing Shapur's triumph over Valerian; the second was at Naqsh-i Rajab, near a carving showing the god Ahura Mazda presenting the symbols of power to the first Sassanid King of Kings, Ardashir *(Plates 126, 129);* and the third (discovered by Herzfeld in 1926) was at Sar Mashhad, near Kazerun, above a carving in which Varahran II was shown killing a lion with a sword. But of these inscriptions only one—the shortest, at Naqsh-i Rajab—could be read: the others were full of lacunae. The discovery of a new inscription by Kartir on the plinth of the "Kaaba of Zoroaster" made it possible to fill the gaps.

From the inscriptions we obtain a clear picture of the important part played by the chief priest of the country under the early Sassanids—all the inscriptions by Kartir date from the reign of Varahran II. As we have already noted, he was able to make kings or to destroy them as he pleased. The inscriptions record his dizzy rise from being a humble temple priest to become the chief priest of the whole country, the religious teacher and spiritual adviser (the "soul-keeper") of the King of Kings, and the "governor" of the dynastic temple of Anahita, the Kaaba of Zoroaster. In his inscriptions Kartir recounts his various achievements. It was he who forcibly established the cult of fire and Zoroastrianism, the "creed of those who worship Ahura Mazda", in all the conquered areas; it was to him that the Sassanian empire owed the transformation of Zoroastrianism into the state religion; it was he who achieved throughout Persian territory the suppression of Christians, Manichaeans, Buddhists and other worshippers of the *daêvas,* and the destruction of their temples. The inscriptions also set out his creed—the authentic doctrine of Zoroastrianism which he declared to be the accepted canon. But it is precisely at this point in the inscriptions that it is almost impossible to restore the text, and so we do not know what was contained in Kartir's *Avesta,* or precisely what dogmas he proclaimed as the true faith. What makes all this more interesting still is that none of the later sources mention this man who left these four lengthy inscriptions in the very place which before and after his time was reserved for inscriptions and carvings by the King of Kings. In later years, indeed, the Sassanian priests actually invented a mythical religious leader to whom they gave the name of Tosar. In the 6th century, three hundred years after the time of Kartir, there appeared a tendentious forgery, the so-called "Letter of Tosar". According to this document Tosar had been chief priest in the time of the early Sassanid kings, and had bent all his energies to glorifying the slightest actions of the kings of Iran, declaring them to be "God's design". This Tosar, with his tedious sermons about the "goodness" of the rulers of Iran, was a very different person from Kartir, the overthrower of thrones, the merciless fanatic, the leader of the court faction, who for more than a quarter of a century had controlled the destinies of the country. Archaeology helps us to understand what actually happened; and in particular, by studying the extant remains, we can get some idea of the Zoroastrian doctrines which Kartir established as the orthodox creed.

Until the seventies of the 3rd century—the period of Kartir's activity—Sassanian court art was almost entirely confined to official portraits and representations of the principal Zoroastrian divinities—Ahura Mazda, Mithra and Anahita—created in the image of the King of Kings of Iran. In the reign of Varahran II, the ruler who was raised to the throne by Kartir and was wholly under his influence, we have the dish found at Nizhne-Shakhorovka which has already been discussed and the representations of various animals on the coins. The range of such representations, however, is extremely limited. On all the works belonging to this period we find only figures of horses, bulls, wild boars, lions, the Senmurw and the bird Varagn. It is probably correct to associate their appearance in the official art of Iran with Kartir's religious reform, and to suppose that the texts which were declared to contain the true faith included those which mention the divinities Verethragna (represented, as we have already noted, in the form of a horse, a bird and a wild boar), Tishtrya (in the form of a horse), the "primal ox" (the humped ox), the Senmurw, Mithra (in the form of a lion) and some others. A sentence in one of Kartir's inscriptions now becomes comprehensible: "And he who shall see and read this inscription,... may he believe more firmly in these *yashts* (religious hymns) and these (religious) acts and this faith which have now become established, and may he not be in thrall to any others. And may he know that there are the heavens above and there is the abyss of hell. And may he who has chosen to follow the true doctrine (i.e., the school of Zoroastrian thought advocated by Kartir) go to heaven, and he who has chosen to follow evil (i.e., other Zoroastrian doctrines) be cast down into the abyss of hell."

The exact dating of the seals—the field of Sassanian art which shows the greatest variety of subject—has demonstrated that the range of symbolic figures changed with the passage of time. In Iranian art of the time of Kartir and Varahran II we find no trace of the symbols of Anahita which are so common from the 4th century onwards—various flowers, pomegranates, a dove, a peacock, and the naked dancing girls who were Anahita's priestesses, bearing these symbols in their hands. In the 3rd century Anahita was identified with the Queen of Queens of Iran, and the "governor" of her temple was Kartir. We know from the religious texts that thirty years later, after Kartir's death, the King of Kings Shapur II caused the shrines of Anahita to be renewed and rebuilt.

At that time Shapur II's chief priest Aturpat, who was engaged in the same task as Kartir had undertaken only thirty years before—the editing of the text of the *Avesta*—transformed the nature of the cult of Anahita, associating the goddess more closely with the worship of vegetation, of water, of flowers. It was probably also this period that saw the production of the splendid silver water jugs with the figures of Anahita's priestesses, the dancing girls carrying flowers and fruits in their hands *(Plates 172, 181, 183–189, 195)*.

In the art of Iran during the period of Kartir and Varahran II we find no trace of the figure, which was later to become so popular, of a leaping mountain ram with an elaborate bow round its neck—the symbol of the god of success and the imperial glory, Hvarnah. This symbol first appears in the time of Shapur II and Aturpat on the military helmet of the Shahanshah (as described by Ammianus Marcellinus), in numerous works of art, and in literature *(Plates 144, 159, 202)*. The *yashts* about Hvarnah, which played little part in Kartir's *Avesta*, figure prominently in the *Avesta* of Aturpat.

It was no accident that these themes came into use in the 4th century. This was the time when, for a variety of political reasons, there was invented a false genealogy of the Sassanid Shahanshahs, tracing their ancestry back to the Kayanids, the ancient kings of the Persian national epic; and this was the time, too, when Shapur II's secretary Khorkhbud composed on the king's instructions a chronicle called the "Veracious Account". This document, which was not remarkable for its veracity, told how the "good fortune of Hvarnah of the Kayanids" (the divinity of the imperial glory) watched over the first Sassanid king in the form of a ram with an elaborate ribbon bow round its neck and ensured his victory over the Parthians.

Thus thirty years after his death Kartir had become a heretic in the eyes of the Zoroastrian priests, and all he had achieved in the field of religion was deliberately forgotten. The King of Kings of Iran could no longer allow so much power to be concentrated in the hands of one man: the events associated with the overthrow of Narseh, referred to on an earlier page, had shown what this might lead to. Shapur II's priest Aturpat, whom all the Zoroastrian texts declare to be the supreme religious authority, cleansed Zoroastrianism of its alleged impurities and regenerated it; and Kartir's name disappeared from the pages of the religious chronicles and the historical records. The half obliterated inscriptions and the remains discovered by the archaeologists have helped us to reconstruct the course of his activity and revealed the stages of development of Zoroastrianism, presenting the historians of the early Middle Age of Iran with a new and fascinating problem —the problem of the relationships of throne and altar.

← 195

196 197

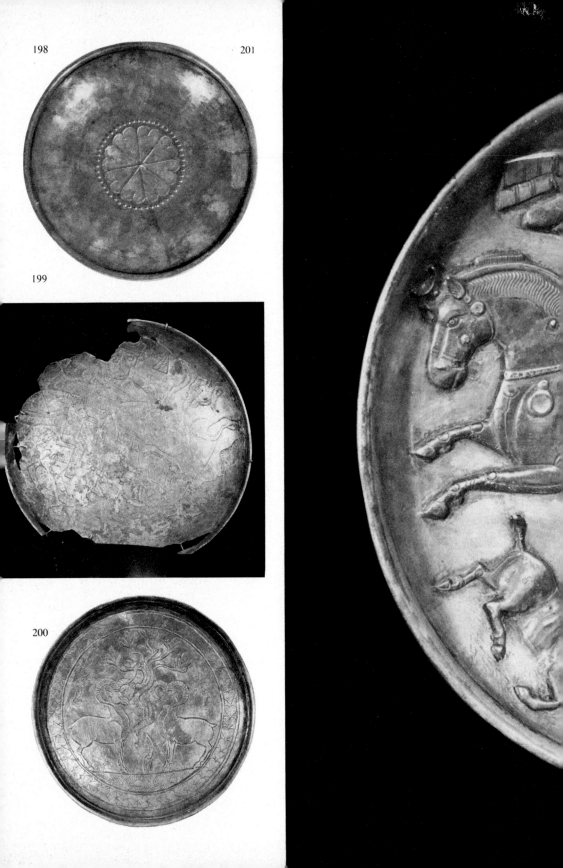

198

201

199

200

203　　　　　　202

206

208

211

209

210

← 212

213

214

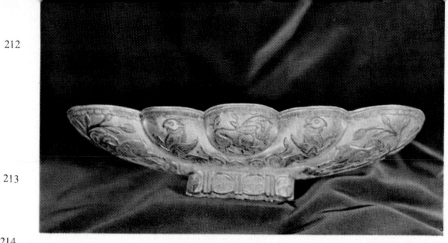

215

216

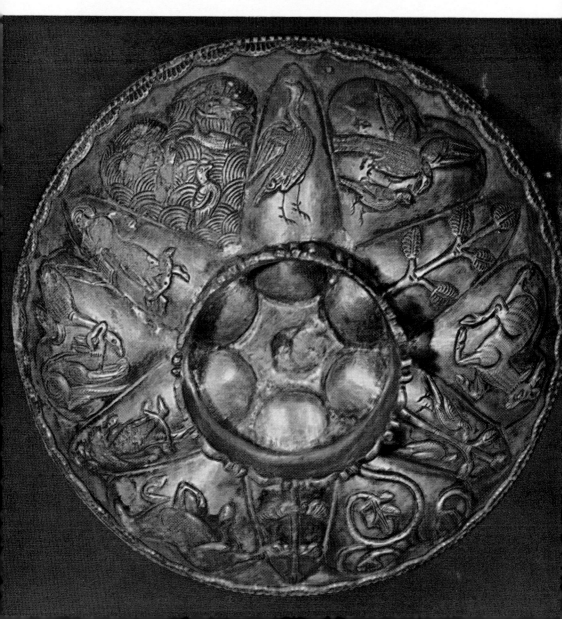

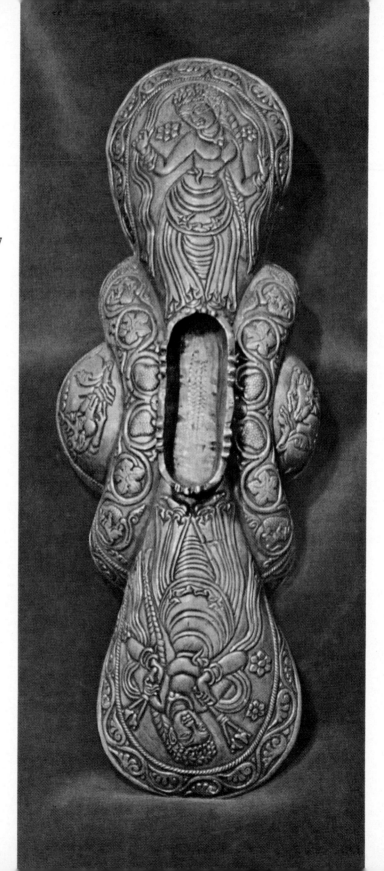

CONCLUSION

In this brief study it would have been impossible to find room for an account of the civilisation of Iran during a period of almost a thousand years—years, too, so full of stirring events. I have not, therefore, made any attempt to do so. The story of Iran between the 3rd century B.C. and the 7th century A.D. as told in this book is not complete. Nor is it complete in archaeology: we are faced with too many problems which still await a solution, too many areas which have not yet undergone archaeological investigation, too many objects which have not yet been satisfactorily dated or interpreted. A period of fifty years—which is roughly the time that has elapsed since the first large-scale investigations of the culture of Iran in the Hellenistic period and early Middle Age—is not, I think, sufficient to allow us to hazard any generalisations or to regard the conclusions so far reached as definitive. The future undoubtedly holds many surprises. The urgent need, in present circumstances, is to carry out further excavations on the territory of Iran.

CHRONOLOGICAL TABLE

B.C.	Seleucids	Parthians	Rome
	Seleucus I Nicator 312-281		First Punic War 263–241
	Antiochus I Soter 281–261		
	Antiochus II Theos 261–246	Arshak (Arsaces) in Parthyene, c. 250	
	Seleucus II Callinicus 246–225	Arshak proclaimed king, 238	
	Seleucus III Soter 225–223	Arsaces I 238–210	Second Punic War 218–201
	Antiochus III 223–187	Arsaces II 210–191	
	Seleucus IV Philopator 187–175	Phriapatius 191–176	
	Antiochus IV Epiphanes 175–163	Phraates I 176–171 Mithridates I, the Great 171–138	
	Antiochus V Eupator 163–162		
		Phraates II c. 138–128	
		Artabanus I c. 128–123	
		Mithridates II, King of Kings c. 123–87	
		Orodes I 80–76	
		Phraates III 70–58	First Triumvirate (Caesar, Pompey, Crassus), 60–53
		Orodes II 56–37	Battle of Carrhae, 53
		Phraates IV c. 40–2	

Parthians	Rome
Phraates V	Augustus
2 B.C.- 4 A.D.	27 B.C.-14 A.D.
A.D. Orodes III	
4–7	
Vonones I	
8/9–11/12	
Artabanus II	
c. 10–38	
Gotarzes II – – Vardanes	
40/41–51 38–47	
Valarsh (Vologeses) I	
51–79/80	Nero
	57–68
Artabanus III	
80-81	
Khusro (Osroes)	Trajan
106/107–129	98–117
Valarsh (Vologeses) IV	First Parthian War
147/148–192	114–117
	Marcus Aurelius
	161–180
	Second Parthian War
	161–166
Valarsh (Vologeses) V	Septimius Severus
c. 191–207	193–211
	Campaigns in the East
	197–202
Artabanus IV – – Valarsh (Vologeses) VI	
213–227 (?) 207–223 (?)	
Artavasdes	
227–229 (?)	

Sassanids	Rome
	Severan Dynasty 193–235
Ardashir I 227–243	Alexander Severus at war with Ardashir, 235 The Soldier Emperors 235–251
Shapur I 243–273 **Hormizd Ardashir** 274 **Varahran I** 274–276	Valerian at war with Shapur, 256 Valerian taken prisoner by Shapur, 260
Varahran II 276–293 **Narseh** 293–302	**Diocletian** 284–305
Hormizd II 302–309 **Shapur II** 309–379	**Constantine the Great** 305–337
Ardashir II 379–383 **Shapur III** 383–388	*Byzantium*
Yazdagird I 399–420 **Varahran V** 420–438	**Arcadius** 395–408 **Theodosius II** 408–450
Yazdagird II 438–457 **Hormizd III** 457–459 **Peroz** 457–483	**Zeno** 474–491

Sassanids	_Byzantium_
Valash 484–488	
Kavad 488–531	Anastasius I 491–518
Khusro I 531–579	Justin I 518–527
Hormizd IV 579–590	Justinian 527–565
Varahran VI 590–591	
Khusro II 591–628	Phocas 602–610
Yazdagird III 632–651	Heraclius 610–641

BIBLIOGRAPHY

General Works

G. CONTENAU, *Arts et styles de l'Asie antérieure*. Paris, 1948.

F. CUMONT, *Recherches sur le symbolisme funéraire des Romains*. Paris, 1924.

M. DIEULAFOY, *L'art antique de la Perse (Achéménides, Parthes, Sassanides)*. Paris, 1884.

E. FLANDIN, P. COSTE, *Voyage en Perse pendant les années 1840-1842*. Paris, 1843–1854 (6 vols).

R. GHIRSHMAN, *Persian Art: the Parthian and Sassanian Dynasties*. London and New York, 1962.

R. GHIRSHMAN, *Iran: from the earliest times to the Islamic conquest*. Penguin Books, 1954.

A. GODARD, *The Art of Iran*. London, 1965.

E. HERZFELD, *Am Tor von Asien*. Berlin, 1920.

E. HERZFELD, *Archaeological History of Iran*. London, 1935.

E. HERZFELD, *Iran in the Ancient East*. London and New York, 1941.

A.U. POPE (ed.), *A Survey of Persian Art*. London and New York, 1938 (6 vols.).

E. PORADA, *Ancient Iran*. "Art of the World", London, 1965.

F. SARRE, E. HERZFELD, *Iranische Felsreliefs*. Berlin, 1910.

SIR AUREL STEIN, "An Archaeological Tour in the Ancient Persis", *Iraq*, III, 1936, 2.

SIR AUREL STEIN, *Old Routes of Western Iran*. London, 1940.

R. FRYE, *The Heritage of Persia*. London, 1962.

L. VANDEN BERGHE, *Archéologie de l'Iran ancien*. Leyden, 1959.

L. VANDEN BERGHE, H.F. MUSSCHE, *Bibliographie analytique de l'assyriologie et de l'archéologie du Proche-Orient*. Vol. I, *L'archéologie, 1954-1955*. Leyden, 1956.

Seleucid and Parthian Iran
General Works

N. DEBEVOISE, *A Political History of Parthia*. Chicago, 1938.

J.G. DROUSEN, *Geschichte des Hellenismus*, Bd I-II. Basle, 1952.

A.B. RANOVICH, *Ellinizm i ego istoricheskaya rol* ("The Hellenistic world and its historical significance"). Moscow, 1950.

M.I. ROSTOVTZEFF, *The Social and Economic History of the Hellenistic World*, Vols. I-III. Oxford, 1941.

SIR WILLIAM TARN, G.T. GRIFFITH, *Hellenistic Civilisation*. London, 1959.

G. WIDENGREN, *Iranisch-semitische Kulturbegegnung in der parthischen Zeit*. Cologne, 1960.

Archaeology
   Dura-Europos, Hatra

F. CUMONT, *Fouilles de Doura-Europos*. Paris, 1926.

M.I. ROSTOVTZEFF, "Dura and the Problem of Parthian Art", *Yale Classical Studies*, V, 1935.

Excavations at Dura-Europos: Preliminary Reports, I-IX, New Haven, 1929-1955; Final Reports, III, V, VIII, New Haven, 1956-1959.

W. ANDRAE, *Hatra*, I. Leipzig, 1908; *Hatra*, II. Leipzig, 1912.

D. HOMES-FREDERICQ, *Hatra et ses sculptures parthes. Etude stylistique et iconographique*. Istanbul, 1963.

H. INGHOLT, "Parthian Sculptures from Hatra (Orient and Hellas in Art and Religion)", *Memoirs of the Connecticut Academy of Sciences*, XII, July 1954.

   Nisa, Merv

Trudy yuzhno-turkmenskoy arkheologicheskoy ekspeditsii ("Reports of the Southern Turkmenian Archaeological Expedition"), I-V. Ashkhabad, 1949-1955.

M.E. MASSON, G.A. PUGACHENKOVA, *Ritony Nisy* ("The rhytons from Nisa"). Ashkhabad, 1959.

Sassanian Iran
General Works

T. NÖLDEKE, *Geschichte der Perser und Araber zur Zeit der Sassaniden. Aus der arabischen Chronik des Tabari übersetzt und mit ausführlichen Erläuterungen und Ergänzungen versehen*. Leyden, 1879.

A. CHRISTENSEN, *L'Iran sous les Sassanides*. Copenhagen, 1944.

F. ALTHEIM, R. STIEHL, *Ein asiatischer Staat*. Vol. I. Wiesbaden, 1954.

E. HONIGMAN, A. MARICQ, "Recherches sur les *Res Gestae Divi Saporis*", *Mémoires de l'Académie Royale de Belgique, Classe des lettres*, XLVII, 4. Brussels, 1953.

N. PIGULEVSKAJA, *Les villes de l'état iranien aux époques parthe et sassanide*. Paris, 1963.

Archaeology, Works of Art

A. BORISOV, V. LUKONIN, *Sassanidskie Gemmy* ("Sassanian gems"). Leningrad, 1963.

K. ERDMANN, "Zur Chronologie der sassanidischen Kunst", *Forschungen und Fortschritte*, XIII, 1937.

K. ERDMANN, *Die Kunst Irans zur Zeit der Sassaniden*. Berlin, 1943.

R. GHIRSHMAN, "Cinq campagnes de fouilles à Suse", *Revue d'assyriologie et d'archéologie orientale*, XLVI, 1952.

R. GHIRSHMAN, *Bîchâpour*, Vol. II, *Les mosaïques sassanides*. Musée du Louvre, Paris, 1956.

E. HERZFELD, "Der Thron des Khosro", *Jahrbuch der preussischen Kunstsammlungen*, 41, 1920.

E. HERZFELD, "Khusrau Parwez und der Taq i Vastan", *Archäologische Mitteilungen aus Iran*, IX, 1938.

P. HORN, G. STEINDORFF, *Sassanidische Siegelsteine*. Berlin, 1896.

G. INOSTRANTSEFF, *Sassanidskie Etyudy (Etudes sassanides)*. St Petersburg, 1909.

H. LENZEN, "Zur relativen Chronologie der sassanidischen Stuckarbeiten", *Jahrbuch des deutschen archäologischen Instituts*, 67, 1952.

V. LUKONIN, *Iran v epokhu pervikh Sassanidov* ("Iran under the early Sassanids") Leningrad, 1961.

J. DE MORGAN, *Mission scientifique en Perse: Recherches archéologiques*. Vol. IV. Paris, 1896.

J. ORBELI, C. TREVER, *Orfèvrerie sassanide*. Moscow and Leningrad, 1935.

H.H. VON DER OSTEN, R. NAUMANN, *Takht-i Sulaimân*, Bd I. Berlin, 1961.

J. SMIRNOV, *Vostochnoe serebro (Argenterie orientale)*. St Petersburg, 1909.

C. TREVER, *Nouveaux plats sassanides de l'Ermitage*. Moscow and Leningrad, 1937.

Special Questions

Language and Literature in Parthian and Sassanian Iran

W. B. HENNING, *Mitteliranisch.* (*Handbuch der Orientalistik*, Erste Abteilung, Bd IV, Abschn. I). Leyden and Cologne, 1958 (with bibliography).

J. HARMATTA, "The Parthian Parchment from Dura-Europos", *Acta Antiqua Hungaricae*, V, 1957.

F. ALTHEIM, R. STIEHL, *Supplementum Aramaicum: Aramäisches aus Iran.* Baden-Baden, 1957.

I. DYAKONOV, V. LIVSHITS, *Dokumenty iz Nisy I v. do n.e.* ("Documents from Nisa of the lst century B.C."). Moscow, 1960.

V. LIVSHITS, *Dokumenty s gory Mug* ("Documents from Mount Mug"). Moscow, 1963.

V. LIVSHITS, V. LUKONIN, "Srednepersidskie i sogdiiskie nadpisi na torevtike" ("Middle Persian and Sogdian inscriptions on silver vessels"). *Vestnik drevney istorii*, 3, 1964.

Corpus Inscriptionum Iranicarum, Part III, Vol. II, Portfolio I (1955); Portfolio III (1963).

Kushan and Kushano-Sassanion Coins; Techniques of Numismatic Study

A. CUNNINGHAM, "Later Indo-Scythians", *Numismatic Chronicle*, Ser. III, Vol. XIII, 1895.

R. GÖBL, "Die Münzprägung der Kušan von Vima Kadphises bis Bahram IV", in F. Altheim and R. Stiehl, *Finanzgeschichte der Spätantike*, Frankfurt am Main, 1957, pp. 173-257.

R. GÖBL, "Zwei neue Termini für ein zentrales Datum der alten Geschichte Mittelasiens, das Jahr I des Kušankönigs Kaniška", *Anzeiger der phil.-hist. Klasse der Österreichischen Akademie der Wissenschaften zu Wien*, 1964.

R. GHIRSHMAN, "Le problème de la chronologie des Kouchans", *Cahiers d'histoire mondiale*, III, 1957.

R. GHIRSHMAN, "Les Chionites-Hephtalites", *MDAFA*, XIII, 1948.

E. ZEYMAL, *Problema kushanskoy Khronologii i Monety* ("The problem of Kushan chronology and the coins"). *Doklady na yubileynoy sessii Gosudarstvennogo Ermitazha*. Leningrad, October 1964.

E. ZEYMAL, *Kushanskoe Tsarstvo po monetnym dannym* ("The Kushan kingdom on the evidence of the coins"). Leningrad, 1965.

E. HERZFELD, "Kushano-Sasanian Coins", *Memoirs of the Archaeological Survey of India*, No. 38. Calcutta, 1930.

R. CURIEL, "Le trésor du Tépé Maranjan", *MDAFA*, XIV, 1953.

A. D. BIVAR, "The Kushano-Sassanian Coin Series", *Journal of the Numismatic Society of India*, XVIII, i, 1956.

V. LUKONIN, "K voprosu o kushano-sassanidskikh monetakh" ("Kushano-Sassanian coins"). *Epigrafika Vostoka*, XVIII, 1966.

Sassanian Coins and Sassanian History

E. HERZFELD, *Paikuli: Monuments and Inscriptions of the Early History of the Sassanian Empire*, Vols. I-II. Berlin, 1924.

R. GÖBL, "Aufbau der Münzprägung", in F. Altheim and R. Stiehl, *Ein asiatischer Staat*, Wiesbaden, 1954, pp. 51–128.

W. B. HENNING, "A Farewell to the Khagan of the Aq-Aqatārân", *BSOAS*, XIV, 1952.

R. FRYE, "Remarks on Paikuli and Sar-Mashad Inscriptions", *HJAS*, 20, 1957.

V. LUKONIN, "Varahran II, Narse", *Vestnik drevney istorii*, 1, 1964.

The Development of Religions in Iran; the Religious Koiné; the Problem of Frontality; Religion and Art; Zoroastrianism

N. S. NYBERG, *Die Religionen des Alten Iran*. Leipzig, 1938.

R. C. ZAEHNER, *Zurvan: a Zoroastrian Dilemma*. Oxford, 1955.

J. M. UNVALA, *Observations on the Religion of the Parthians*. Bombay, 1925.

S. WIKANDER, *Die Feuerpriester in Kleinasien und Iran*. Lund, 1946.

E. WILL, *Le relief cultuel gréco-romain*. Paris, 1955.

H. SEYRIG, "Antiquités syriennes", *Syria*, XVIII, 1937.

H. SEYRIG, "Note sur le style des bas-reliefs", *Syria*, XV, 1934.

D. SCHLUMBERGER, "Descendants non-méditerranéens de l'art grec", *Syria*, XXXVII, 1960.

S. HOPKINS, "A Note on Frontality in Near Eastern Art", *Ars Islamica*, III, 1936.

M. I. ROSTOVTZEFF, "L'art gréco-iranien", *Revue des arts asiatiques*, VII.

F. CUMONT, "Les bronzes gréco-parthes de Shami", *Syria*, XX, 1939.

G. KOSHELENKO, "Frontalnost v parfyanskom iskusstve" ("Frontality in Parthian art"), *Vestnik drevney istorii*, 3, 1963.

V. LUKONIN, "Les monnaies d'Artashir I", *Iranica Antiqua*, VI, 1967.

V. LUKONIN, "Kartir i Mani" ("Kartir and Mani"), *Vestnik drevney istorii*, 3, 1966.

LIST OF ILLUSTRATIONS

(Unless otherwise indicated, all the objects illustrated in this book are in the Hermitage Museum, Leningrad).

18 *Parthian art. Bust of a Parthian prince. Emblem in silver. Weight 164 g. Dimensions 15.8 × 11 cm. 2nd century A.D.*

19 *Parthian art. Bronze figurine. Kurdistan. (Archaeological Museum, Baghdad).*

20 *Hellenistic art. Aphrodite (?). Marble. 2nd century B.C. Nisa.*

21 *Parthian art. Bronze statuette. 3rd–2nd century B.C. Shami. (Archaeological Museum, Teheran).*

22 *Hellenistic art. Bronze statuette. Nihavend. (Archaeological Museum, Teheran).*

23 *Hellenistic art. Statuette of Athene. Bronze. Nihavend. (Archaeological Museum, Teheran).*

24 *Parthian art. Bust of a child. Pottery. 1st–2nd century A.D. Susa. (Archaeological Museum, Teheran).*

25 *Hellenistic art. Head of a Parthian queen. Marble. End of 1st century B.C. Susa (Archaeological Museum, Teheran).*

26 *Hellenistic art. Silver vase with handles. Parthian period. (Archaeological Museum, Teheran).*

27 *Hellenistic art. Silver bowl (exterior), decorated with a Gorgon's head. Weight 244.5 g. Diameter 12 cm. 2nd–1st century B.C.*

28 *Parthian or Sassanian art. Flute-player. Fresco. 3rd century A.D. Kuh-i Khwaja.*

29 *Parthian art. Antiochus I of Commagene and Apollo-Mithra. Drawing of a carving at Nimrud Dagh. 69–34 B.C.*

30 *Hellenistic art. Handle decorated with face. Bronze. Parthian period. 2nd century A.D. (Archaeological Museum, Teheran).*

31 *Hellenistic art. Gold vase with two handles. Weight 455.5 g. Diameter 12 cm. Height 13 cm. 3rd–2nd century B.C.*

32 *Parthian or Sassanian art. Figurine of a boar. Gold. 2nd–3rd century A.D.*

33 *Parthian art. Gold plate. Weight 284.2 g. Diameter 19 cm. 1st–2nd century A.D.*

34 *Parthian art. Detail of a silver vase. On the base, inscription in Aramaic. 1st century A.D. Bori, Georgia.*

35 *Greco-Bactrian art. Silver emblem, partly gilded (central medaillon from interior of silver dish), with figure of Artemis. Weight 197 g. Diameter 10 cm.*

36 *Greco-Bactrian art. Silver emblem, partly gilded (central medallion from interior of silver dish), with figure of the goddess Khvaninda. Weight 53.5 g. Diameter 12 cm.*

37 *Sassanian art. Silver plate decorated with sacred animals. 3rd century A.D. On the reverse is a Sogdian inscription of the 6th–7th century A.D.*
Transliteration: čn pr(?)nč
III C(?)X
Translation: *"(Belonging) to Farnch. (Weight) 310"*

38 *Eastern Hellenistic art (Greco-Bactrian style?). Silver phalera, partly gilded. Weight 404.2 g. Diameter 24 cm.*

39 *Hellenistic art. Silver cup, partly gilded, decorated with heads of goddesses. Weight 230.5 g. Diameter 14 cm. 2nd–1st century B.C.*

40 *Eastern Hellenistic art (Greco-Bactrian style?). Silver phalera, partly gilded. Weight 407.9 g. Diameter 24 cm.*

41 *Hellenistic art. Silver phalera, partly gilded. Weight 634.7 g. Diameter 25 cm.*

42 *Hellenistic art. Silver phalera, partly gilded. Weight 627 g. Diameter 25 cm.*

43 *Hellenistic art. Gold cup. Weight 677.5 g. Diameter 16 cm. Height 8 cm. 2nd century B.C. Round the upper border is an Aramaic inscription of the 2nd century B.C.*
Transliteration: K III III III Q I III I III MN kryhw(?)
Translation: *"(Belonging) to Kryhv(?). Weight (or value) K 9, Q 8"*
(K and Q being abbreviations for weights or measures).

44 *Hellenistic art. Glass cup made of two vessels fitted into one another, with a leaf pattern in gold between them. 3rd–2nd century B.C. Syria.*

45 *Hellenistic or Parthian art. Gold cup. Weight 181.5 g. Diameter 13 cm. Height 5 cm.*

46 *Cup of ruby glass with decoration in silver appliqué. 4th century A.D. Syria(?). Found in the Mtskheta Tomb, Georgia.*

47 *Parthian art. Jewellery.*
(above, left and right) Earrings. 1st–2nd century A.D.
(centre) Earring, bearing the name of its owner, Autophradates. 1st–2nd century A.D.
(below) Belt buckle. 1st century A.D.

48 *Parthian art. Belt buckle decorated with an intaglio representing the god Mithra. 2nd–3rd century A.D.*

49 *Gold coin of the Kushan king Kanishka. Reverse: the goddess Anahita (Nanaia). 3rd century A.D.(?).*

50 *Gold coin of the Kushan king Vasudeva. 4th century A.D.(?).*

51 *Drachma of the Parthian king Valarsh (Vologeses) III (147/148–192 A.D.).*

52 *Parthian drachma with the head of Arshak (Arsaces), son of Tiridates I (210–191 B.C.).*

53 *Drachma of the Parthian king Orodes I (80–76 B.C.).*

54 *Drachma with the head of Musa, wife of the Parthian king Phraates IV (2 B.C.–4 A.D.).*

55 *Parthian art. Seal of Antiochus. 2nd–3rd century A.D.*

56 *Hellenistic art. Seal decorated with three horses. 4th–3rd century B.C.*

57 *Seal with Gopat Shah, the Zoroastrian divinity of water. 4th century B.C.*

58 *Greco-Persian art. Seal with scene of fighting. 4th century B.C.*

59 *Sassanian art. Seal of the Queen of Queens Denak, wife of Ardashir I. Pahlavi inscription of 3rd century A.D.*
Transliteration: *dynky ZY MLKT'n MLKT' mhy*
sty PWN tny š'pstn (or, better: š'pst'n)
Translation: *"The chief eunuch of the Queen of Queens, Denak"; or, with the reading š'pst'n: "Denak, Queen of Queens, first lady of the harem".*

60 *Sassanian art. Seal of Papak, governor of the city of Khosrav-Shat Hormizd. 4th century A.D. Pahlavi inscription of 4th century.*

Transliteration: *p'pky ZY hwsrw (. . .) 'whrmz(dy) (št)rpy*
Translation: *"Papak, governor of the city of Khosrav-Shat Hormizd"*.

61 *Sassanian seal. A chief priest. 3rd–4th century A.D.*

62 *Sassanian seal. The chief priest Khusro, son of Aturfarnbag. 4th century A.D. Pahlavi inscription of 4th century.*
Transliteration: *hwslwy ZY mgw ZY 'twrprnbg'n*
Translation: *"Khusro, son of Aturfarnbag"*

63 *Sassanian seal with head of a chief priest. 3rd century A.D.*

64 *Sassanian seal with head of a prince or high official. 3rd century A.D.*

65 *Sassanian seal with head of a princess. 3rd century A.D.*

66 *Cf. No. 62.*

67 *Sassanian seal. A noble named Vyst. 3rd century A.D. Parthian inscription of early Sassanian period.*
Transliteration: *lw'gn wyst mrtpty*
Translation: *"Lyvagn Vyst(?), master of the household"*

68 *Sassanian seal with head of a chief priest or high official. 4th century A.D. Pahlavi inscription of 4th century.*
Transliteration: *mtr m'hy 'whrmzd'n*
Translation: *"Mihrmah, son of Hormizd"*

69 *Sassanian seal with head of a noble named Hormizd Varaz. 4th century A.D. Pahlavi inscription of 4th century.*
Transliteration: *wr'č 'whrmzdy*
Translation: *"Varaz Hormizd"*

70 *Sassanian seal. Portrait of the Roman Emperor Gordian. Roman work, with Pahlavi inscription giving the owner's name: mwštk'y. 3rd century A.D.*

71 *Cf. No. 61.*

72 *Sassanian seal. Gopat Shah, the Zoroastrian divinity of water. 4th–5th century A.D.*

73 *Sassanian seal. Winged griffin. 6th century A.D. Pahlavi inscription.*
Transliteration: *'pst'n 'L yzd'n*
Translation: *"The succour of the gods"*

74 *Sassanian seal. Gopat Shah, the Zoroastrian divinity of water. 4th century A.D. Pahlavi inscription.*

75 *Sassanian seal. Gopat Shah, the Zoroastrian divinity of water. 4th–5th century A.D. Pahlavi inscription.*
Transliteration: *mtly 'pst'n 'L yzd'n*
Translation: *"Mihr: the succour of the gods"*

76 *Sassanian seal. Winged griffin. 6th century A.D. Pahlavi inscription.*

77 *Sassanian seal. Gopat Shah, the Zoroastrian divinity of water. 4th century A.D. Pahlavi inscription.*
Transliteration: *'twrp't*
Translation: "Aturpat" (the owner's name)

78 *Sassanian seal. Gopat Shah, the Zoroastrian divinity of water. 6th century A.D. Pahlavi inscription.*
Transliteration: *'pst'n 'L yzd'n*
Translation: *"The succour of the gods"*

79 *Sassanian seal. Symbolic animal. 6th century A.D. Pahlavi inscription.*
Transliteration: *'pst'n 'L yzd'n*
Translation: *"The succour of the gods"*

80 *Sassanian seal. Symbolic animal. 6th century A.D.*

81 *Sassanian seal. Symbolic animal. 4th century A.D. Pahlavi inscription.*
Transliteration: *'pst'n 'L yzd'n*
Translation: *"The succour of the gods"*

82 *Sassanian seal. Symbolic animal. 4th century A.D.*

83 *Sassanian seal. Symbolic animal. 4th century A.D. Pahlavi inscription.*
Transliteration: *l'styhy p'rswmy*
Translation: *"The divine justice"*

84 *Sassanian seal. Symbolic animal. 4th century A.D. Pahlavi inscription giving the owner's name.*
Transliteration: *mytrm'h šysmyly*

85 *Sassanian seal. Symbolic animal. 5th–6th century A.D.*

86 *Sassanian seal. Symbolic animal. 5th–6th century A.D. Pahlavi inscription.*

87 *Sassanian seal. Symbolic animal. 5th–6th century A.D. Pahlavi inscription.*
Transliteration: *'pzwn*
Translation: "May there be increase (of good fortune)"

88 *Sassanian seal. Symbolic animal. 5th–6th century A.D.*

89 *Sassanian seal. Symbolic animal. 5th–6th century A.D.*

90 *Cf. No. 89.*

91 *Sassanian seal. Symbolic animal. 5th–6th century A.D. Pahlavi inscription.*
Transliteration: *'twr*
Translation: *"Fire (temple)"*

92 *Sassanian seal. Symbolic animal. 5th–6th century A.D.*

93 *Sassanian seal. Symbolic animal. 5th–6th century A.D. Pahlavi inscription giving the owner's name.*
Transliteration: *gwštsp 'whrmzd*

94 *Cf. No. 93.*

95–97 *Sassanian* bullae *with impressions of seals. 6th–7th century A.D. Ak-Tepe, Turkmenia.*

98 *Sassanian seal. Winged griffin attacking an ibex. 6th century A.D.*

99 *Sassanian seal. Symbolic animal. 6th century A.D.*

100 *Sassanian seal. Mahan, a high dignitary. Dimensions 4 × 4 cm. 6th century A.D.*

101 *Sassanian seal. Camel. 6th century A.D. Pahlavi inscription of 6th–7th century giving the owner's name.*
Transliteration: *d'tprn ZY b'rzwšt'n mgw*
Translation: *"Datfarn, son of Barzushtan, priest"*

102 *Cf. No. 67.*

103 *Sassanian seal. An official. 6th century A.D.*

104 *Sassanian coin. Gold denarius of Peroz I. 5th century A.D.*

105 *Sassanian coin. Silver drachma of Puran-duht, daughter of Khusro II (about 632 A.D.).*

132 *Sassanian inscription on the "Kaaba of Zoroaster". 262 A.D.*

133 *Triumph of Shapur I (243–273 A.D.) over the Emperors Valerian and Philip the Arab. About 249 A.D. Carving at Naqsh-i Rustam.*

134 *Victory of Hormizd II (302–309 A.D.) over the Karens. About 302. Carving at Naqsh-i Rustam.*

135 *Sassanian art. Shapur II (309–379 A.D.). Detail from a silver plate, partly gilded.*

136 *Sassanian art. Shapur II (309–379 A.D.). Detail from a silver plate, partly gilded.*

137 *Post-Sassanian art. Prince Pur-i Vahman hunting. Silver plate, partly gilded. Weight 1265.5 g. Diameter 29 cm. On the reverse is a Pahlavi inscription of the 7th century A.D., in three lines.*
Transliteration: *ZNH M'NH pwl y*
　　　　　　　whm'n plmwty kltny
　　　　　　　III C II drmsng
Translation: *"Plate made to the order of Pur-i Vahman. 302 drachmae".*

138 *Sassanian art. Shapur II (309–379 A.D.) hunting lions. Silver plate, partly gilded. Weight 828 g. Diameter 23 cm.*

139 *Sassanian art. Shapur II (309–379 A.D.) hunting wild rams. Silver plate, partly gilded, found in 1912 in the tomb of an Avar prince at Poltava, Ukraine. Weight 628 g. Diameter 23 cm.*

140 *Late Sassanian art. Lion hunt. Silver plate, partly gilded. Weight 1039 g. Diameter 25 cm. On the reverse is a Pahlavi inscription of the 6th–7th century.*
Transliteration: *pylwč'n*
　　　　　　　NPŠH
　　　　　　　IIC XX XX IIII sng
Translation: *"Belongs to Perozan. Weight 244 drachmae".*

141 *Late Sassanian art. Bahram Gur hunting with the girl musician Azadeh (a famous episode from a Sassanian poem, also treated by Firdausi in his Shah-nama). Silver plate, partly gilded. Weight 1155.6 g. Diameter 22 cm. On the reverse is a Pahlavi inscription of the 6th–7th century.*
Transliteration: *sng II C XX XX X III ZWZN'n pylwč'n.*
Translation: *"Weight 253 drachmae. Perozan".*

142 *Late Sassanian art. Bahram Gur hunting with the girl musician Azadeh. Silver plate. Weight 397.5 g. Dimensions 11 × 15 cm. On the reverse is a Pahlavi inscription of the 6th–7th century.*
Transliteration: *mtrbwčyt NPŠH*
        IIC XX XX X ZY(?) ZWZN'n
        sng
Translation: *"Belongs to Mihrbozet. Weight 250 drachmae".*

143 *Sassanian art. Peroz (457–483) hunting wild rams. Silver plate.*

144 *Late Sassanian art. The "Rum", a ram with a ribbon bow round its neck, symbolising Hvarnah, the divinity of the imperial glory. Silver plate. Weight 825 g. Diameter 25 cm.*

145 *Sassanian art. The Senmurw, the dragon-peacock of Iranian mythology. Silver plate, partly gilded. Weight 980.2 g. Diameter 27 cm.*

146 *Post-Sassanian art. Banqueting scene. Silver plate, partly gilded. Weight 959.5 g. Diameter 23 cm.*

147 *Sassanian art. Varahran, "King of the Kushans" (Sassanian viceroy of the eastern provinces), hunting the wild boar. Silver plate, partly gilded. Weight 636 g. Diameter 27.6 cm. On the reverse is a Sogdian inscription, probably of the 5th century.*
Transliteration: *...XXX III IIII styr*
Translation: *"... (name of the owner) 37 staters".*

148 *Sassanian art. Shapur III (383–388 A.D.) killing a leopard. Silver plate, partly gilded. Weight 645 g. Diameter 21.7 cm. On the reverse is a Sogdian inscription of the 7th–8th century A.D.*
Transliteration: *my'rh'w/n č'čnn'pč III III III XX X styrk*
Translation: *"Myarshan (proper name ?) of Shash (in the present-day region of Tashkent). Weight 39 staters".*

149 *Sassanian art. Kavad (488–531 A.D.) or Khusro I (531–579 A.D.) on his throne and hunting wild rams. Silver plate. Weight 985.6 g. Diameter 26 cm. On the reverse is a Hephthalite inscription giving the name and title of the owner.*

150 *Sassanian art. Shapur III (383–388 A.D.). Detail from a silver plate, partly gilded. Cf. No. 148.*

151 *Sassanian art. Hormizd II (302–309 A.D.). Detail from a silver plate, partly gilded. (Cleveland Museum).*

152   *Sogdian art, showing Sassanian influence. Silver ewer, partly gilded, decorated with a winged camel. Weight 2021.5 g. Height 40 cm. 7th–8th century A.D. On the handle is a Chorasmian inscription giving the owner's name and the weight.*

153   *Sassanian art, showing Central Asian influence. Silver cups, partly gilded. 8th century A.D. Eastern Iran.*

154   *Sassanian art. Bucket for* haoma *(a sacred drink). Weight 1384 g. Dimensions 32 × 10 cm.*

155   *Sassanian art, showing Central Asian influence. Silver cups, partly gilded. 8th century A.D. Eastern Iran.*

156   *Sassanian art. Silver cup decorated with flowers and symbolic animals. Weight 239.2 g. 5th–6th century A.D.*

157   *Post-Sassanian art. Silver vase decorated with a deer.*

158   *Late Sassanian or post-Sassanian art. Silver cup decorated with an eagle.*

159   *Sassanian style. Cup with handle, with representation of the "Rum", the symbol of Hvarnah, the divinity of the imperial glory. Silver, partly gilded. 8th century A.D.*

160–161   *Sassanian art. Silver cup. Weight 217.2 g. Diameter 10 cm. 7th century A.D.*

162   *Sassanian art, showing Central Asian influence. Silver cup, partly gilded. 8th century A.D.*

163–164   *Sassanian art, showing Central Asian influence. Silver cup. Weight 453.4 g. Height 9.3 cm. 7th–8th century A.D.*

165   *Sassanian art. Silver ewer, partly gilded, with a figure of the Senmurw, the dragon-peacock of Iranian mythology. Weight 1041 g. Height 32 cm. 6th century A.D.*

166   *Sassanian art. Head of Senmurw(?) in silver, partly gilded. Weight 1090.8 g. Length 60 cm. 5th century A.D.*

167   *Sassanian art. Silver rhyton in the form of a horse's head. (Private collection).*

168   *Sassanian art(?). Pottery jar in the form of a horse. Place of origin uncertain. (Archaeological Museum, Teheran).*

169 *Sassanian art(?). Statuette of a horse. Bronze. Place of origin uncertain. (Archaeological Museum, Teheran).*

170 *Parthian or early Sassanian art. Silver plate decorated with horses. Weight 864.6 g. Diameter 21.1 cm.*

171 *Late Sassanian or post-Sassanian art. Anthropomorphic ewer. Georgia. (Museum of Georgia, Tbilisi).*

172 *Sassanian art. Decorative element from a vase: the goddess Anahita. Silver. Weight 7.5 g. Height 5.8 cm. 5th century A.D.*

173–174 *Late Sassanian art. Perfume-brazier in the form of a horseman. Bronze. Height 35.6 cm.*

175 *Sassanian art. Pottery amphora from Susa.*

176 *Late Sassanian art. Pottery jar.*

177 *Sassanian art. Pottery amphora from Susa.*

178 *Late Sassanian art. Pottery candlestick.*

179 *Sassanian art, Syro-Roman style. Head of musician or dancer. Mosaic at Bishapur. About 270 A.D.*

180 *Sassanian art, Syro-Roman style. Old man. Mosaic at Bishapur. About 270 A.D.*

181 *Sassanian art. The goddess Anahita. Silver dish, partly gilded. 5th–6th century A.D.*

182 *Sassanian art. Silver vase, partly gilded, decorated with a human face. Weight 358.35 g. Height 14 cm. 5th–6th century A.D.*

183 *Sassanian art. Silver vase, partly gilded, with figures of priestesses of Anahita. Weight 116.9 g. Height 12 cm. 5th–6th century A.D. On the base are Pahlavi and Sogdian inscriptions of the 6th–7th century.*
Transliteration: *(Pahlavi) sng ZY (?) IIC III III ZWZN W M*
             (Sogdian) m(?)δrk'
Translation: *(Pahlavi) "206 drachmae and 3 dangs" (1 dang = 1/6 drachma).*
             (Sogdian) "Mithrak" (the name of an owner of the vase).

184 *Sassanian art. Silver vase, partly gilded, with figures of priestesses of Anahita. Weight 871.3 g. Height 16.5 cm. 5th–6th century A.D. On the neck is a Sogdian inscription of the 5th–6th century.*

Transliteration: *mš(?)yk xwβ čr'k snky*
    IIC XX XX XX III II rm ptxwr
Translation: *"Charak, prince of Mš(?). Weight 265. Drink always".*

185 *Sassanian art. Priestess of Anahita. Detail. Cf. No. 183.*

186–187 *Sassanian art. Priestesses of Anahita. Details. Cf. Nos. 188 and 189.*

188–189 *Sassanian art. Silver vase, partly gilded, with figures of priestesses of Anahita. 5th century A.D. (Cleveland Museum).*

190 *Sassanian art. Dionysiac scene. Detail from silver cup, partly gilded. 5th century A.D. (Cleveland Museum).*

191–192 *Sassanian art. Silver vase, with* bestiarii *fighting wild beasts. 5th–6th century A.D. (Cleveland Museum).*

193 *The same: detail.*

194 *Sassanian art. Silver vase, partly gilded, with the figure of an eagle, symbolising Verethragna, god of victory. Weight 548.4 g. Height 19 cm. 5th–6th century A.D. On the base is a Pahlavi inscription of the 6th–7th century.*
    Transliteration: *bwlčynwlč y hwslwbn NPŠH MN IIC X III III III ZWZN*
    Translation: *"Belongs to Burzenvarz, son of Khusro. 219 drachmae".*

195 *Late Sassanian art. The bird Garudha holding Anahita, goddess of fruit- fulness, the Zoroastrian symbol of the equinox. Silver plate, partly gilded. Weight 828 g. Diameter 22 cm.*

196 *Late Sassanian art. Lioness giving suck under the sacred tree. Silver plate. Weight 547.5 g. Diameter 20 cm.*

197 *The same: detail.*

198 *Sassanian art. Silver plate decorated with a rosette motif. Weight 1769 g. Diameter 40 cm. 7th century A.D.*

199 *Sassanian art. Varahran VI(?) (590–591 A.D.) hunting lions. Silver plate. Weight 204 g. Diameter 19 cm. 6th century A.D.*

200 *Late Sassanian art. Two rams in front of the sacred tree. Silver plate. Weight 420 g. Diameter 17 cm.*

201 *Sassanian art. Hormizd IV (579–590 A.D.) hunting ibex. Silver plate, partly gilded. Weight 772.5 g. Diameter 20 cm. 6th century A.D.*

202 *Post-Sassanian art. Ibex. Silver plate. 8th century A.D.*

203 *Late Sassianan art. Lioness and sacred tree. Silver plate, partly gilded. Weight 967.35 g. Diameter 23 cm.*

204 *Late Sassanian or post-Sassanian art. Lion pouncing on deer. Silver plate, partly gilded. Weight 1103 g. Diameter 27 cm.*

205 *Late Sassanian art. Sacred birds. Silver plate. Weight 855.2 g. Diameter 22 cm. On the reverse is a Pahlavi inscription of the 6th–7th century.*
Transliteration: *hwslwb*
Translation: *"Khusro" (proper name)*

206 *Sassanian style, showing Central Asian influence. Silver cup. Weight 453.4 g. Height 9.3 cm. 8th century A.D.*

207 *Sassanian art. Silver bowl with figures of Varahran II, his queen and his heir. About 280 A.D. (Museum of Georgia, Tbilisi).*

208 *Sassanian art. The throne of Khusro II (591–628 A.D.), with its famous clockwork mechanism. Silver plate, partly gilded. Weight 985.6 g. Diameter 26 cm.*

209 *Sassanian art. Silver plate, partly gilded, with decoration of scroll-work and birds. Weight 824.4 g. Diameter 20.3 cm. 5th century A.D.*

210 *Sassanian art. Flute-player mounted on a dragon. Silver plate, partly gilded. Weight 459.7 g. Diameter 22 cm. 6th century A.D. On the reserve is a Pahlavi inscription of the 6th–7th century A.D.*
Transliteration: *d'd(?) bwlčmtly y plwhwn y hwslwbn l't y ... NPŠH.*
Translation: *"Belonging to Dadburzmihr, son of Farrohv, grandson of Khusro, town judge..."*

211 *Cf. No. 209: detail. The bird symbolises the good wishes addressed to the owner.*

212 *Cf. No. 204: detail.*

213 *Sassanian art. Silver cup, partly gilded, decorated with symbolic animals. Weight 869.2 g. Dimensions 29 × 12 cm. 6th–7th century A.D.*

214 *Sassanian art. Silver cup, partly gilded (interior). Weight 470 g. Diameter 15 cm. 5th–6th century A.D. Cf. No. 216.*

215 *Sassanian art. Silver cup, partly gilded, decorated on the outside with dionysiac themes. 5th century A.D. (Cleveland Museum).*

216 *Sassanian art. Paradise (harp-player, dancer, animals and sacred trees). Silver cup, partly gilded (exterior). Cf. No. 214.*

217 *Sassanian style of the eastern provinces. Dancing girls and animals. Silver cup, partly gilded (exterior). Weight 663 g. Dimensions 29 × 10 cm. 7th century A.D.*

Photographs

(Figures in italics refer to illustrations)

230

231

PRINTED IN SWITZERLAND

THE TEXT AND ILLUSTRATIONS
IN THIS VOLUME WERE PRINTED
ON THE PRESSES OF NAGEL
PUBLISHERS IN GENEVA.

FINISHED IN MARCH 1967.
BINDING BY NAGEL PHBLISHERS,
GENEVA.

PLATES ENGRAVED BY CLICHÉS UNION, PARIS

LEGAL DEPOSIT No 368

PRINTED IN SWITZERLAND

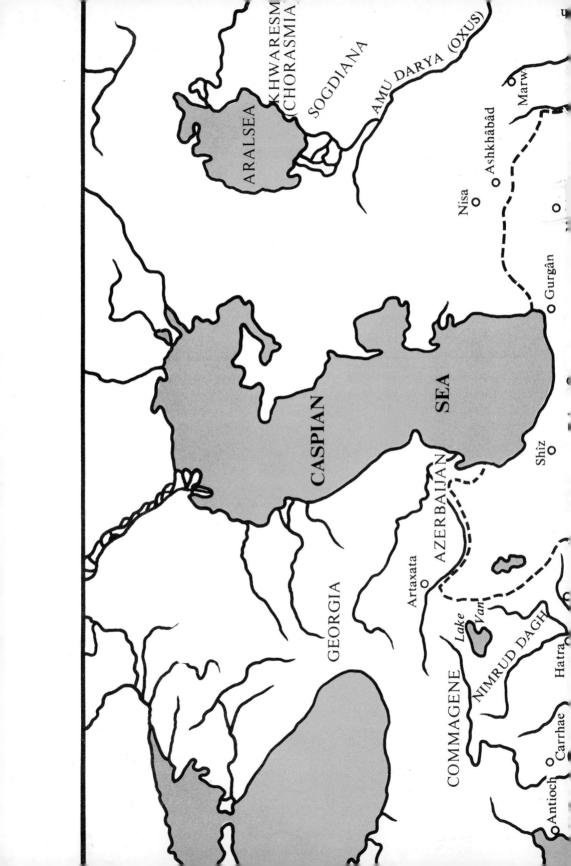